American Philanthropy of the Nineteenth Century

Edited by HERBERT S. BROWN

The Care of Destitute, Neglected and Delinquent Children

The Care of Destitute, Neglected, and Delinquent Children

BY

HOMER FOLKS

*Superintendent of the Children's Aid Society of Pennsylvania, 1890–1893;
Secretary of the New York State Charities Aid Association, 1893–1902;
General Secretary of the National Conference of Charities and Cor-
rection, 1901–1902; Commissioner of Public Charities of the City of
New York, 1902–*

New York

THE MACMILLAN COMPANY

LONDON: MACMILLAN & CO., LTD.

1902

NASW Classics Series

National Association of Social Workers, Inc.
1425 H Street, N W
Washington, D.C. 20005

HV
881
.F63
1978

5-8-80

PREFACE

THE purpose of the present series is to bring to bear on the practical problems of American social workers a concise knowledge of the historical evolution through which the charities of the country have passed. The classification of the subject adopted in the series follows approximately the historical order. At the beginning of the nineteenth century and in the earlier colonial days the almshouse, half retributive, wholly uncharitable, stood (aside from a still cruder system of outdoor relief copied from the English poor law) practically the sole institutional representative of society's interest in its helpless members. In time, however, hospitals for the segregation of the mentally defective on the one hand, and for the general treatment of the sick on the other, began to care for some who hitherto had been sheltered, if at all, in the almshouse; while the elaboration of the penal system of the country effected a somewhat more complete differentiation between pauper and criminal, and introduced the latter as a special object of philanthropic interest. At the same time the needs and rights of dependent childhood began to receive wider recognition by the establishment of institutions and societies for children. Later on in the century the home, which as a relief centre antedates the almshouse, became the focus of a new interest, as the proper centre of a reconstructive and preventive social effort which has since grown in complexity and magnitude to overshadow and to dominate, with its determination to treat causes rather than results, the whole field of philanthropy. In this progress, from the catch-all primitive almshouse, through the elaborate specialization of palliative charity which has characterized the century, into the era of preventive effort which marks its close, there has been need of unremitting supervision, to conserve in their true spirit the charitable ideals for which our existing institutions and systems stand, and of persistent educational work, to arouse and maintain the public interest upon which enduring progress in this field is dependent. The classification adopted in the series is, then, as follows: *Institutional care of destitute adults; Defectives: the insane, feeble-minded, and epileptic; Hospitals, dispensaries, and nursing; The treatment of criminals; Destitute, neglected, and delinquent children; Care and relief of needy families; Supervisory and educational movements; Preventive and constructive philanthropy.*

The present volume, in accordance with this classification, is limited to the consideration of the care of children who have been removed from their earlier environment and from parental control, and the direction of whose lives and the burden of whose support has been directly assumed or provided for by public authorities or private charity. Many activities often included under the term "child-saving" will, therefore, not be considered. Nothing will be said, for instance, of movements that are primarily educational, such as day schools, kindergartens, and home libraries. Various agencies which help needy parents to keep their children under their own care, such as day nurseries, are considered in the volume in this series on the care and relief of needy families. Children's hospitals are considered in the volume on hospitals, dispensaries, and nursing; institutions for the training of mentally defective children, in that on the insane, feeble-minded, and epileptic; while the volume on preventive and constructive philanthropy will touch child life at many points not mentioned above.

For the convenience of students who wish to pursue the subject in greater detail, comprehensive lists of authorities have been given in the treatment of each topic considered. But much of the material presented in this series has been collected at first hand, from unpublished records of state boards of charities, institutions, and societies, from masses of legislation as yet not codified or systematized, and from the personal testimony of eye-witnesses and participants in the philanthropic movements of the century. These sources are for the most part inaccessible, except where, as in the case of the present volume, the correspondence and papers accumulated in the preparation of the work have been placed on file, and may be consulted by students of the subjects.

The editor and the writers of the several volumes are indebted to officials and private individuals in all parts of the country for many details of information furnished in the course of this correspondence, at a material expense of labor and persistent research.

THE EDITOR.

CONTENTS

[For a summary of the contents of the individual chapters the reader is referred to the marginal analysis accompanying the text.]

		PAGE
I	Conditions Prevalent at the Opening of the Nineteenth Century . . .	I
II	Public Care of Destitute Children, 1801–1875	12
III	Private Charities for Destitute Children, 1801–1875	43
IV	Removal of Children from Almshouses .	72
V	The State School and Placing-out System	82
VI	The County Children's Home System .	103
VII	The System of Public Support in Private Institutions	115
VIII	The Boarding-out and Placing-out System	150
IX	Laws and Societies for the Rescue of Neglected Children	167
X	Private Charities for Destitute and Neglected Children, 1875–1900 . .	179
XI	Delinquent Children	198
XII	Present Tendencies	239

THE CARE OF DESTITUTE, NEGLECTED, AND DELIN-QUENT CHILDREN

CHAPTER I

CONDITIONS PREVALENT AT THE OPENING OF THE NINETEENTH CENTURY

The best single source of information on the subject-matter of this volume is the report of the committee on the history of child-saving work, C. D. Randall, chairman, presented to the national conference of charities and correction, Chicago, 1893 (Ellis, Boston, out of print; not included in conference proceedings; available in libraries or through members of the committee). The proceedings of the national conference of charities and correction (Ellis, Boston, 1873–) include many valuable papers in addition to those specifically mentioned below. The volume for 1893 contains an index of the preceding volumes. *The Charities Review* (New York, 1891–1901) contains many valuable contributions, — see complete index in last volume. *Charities* (Charity organization society, New York, 1898–) contains much information concerning current events, — index of preceding volumes in volume iv, issue of May 26, 1901. United States bureau of education circular of information No. 6, 1875, relating to reformatory, charitable, and industrial schools for the young, gives statistics and information, with brief account of many institutions, especially reformatories. See also proceedings of the section on the care of dependent,

I

neglected, and wayward children, international congress of charities, correction, and philanthropy, Chicago, 1893 (Johns Hopkins press, Baltimore); Warner, "American charities" (Crowell, New York, 1894), chapter ix; and Henderson, "Dependents, defectives, and delinquents" (Heath, Boston, 1901), chapter vii. An alphabetical list of the authorities referred to in the present volume, together with numerous other references on the general subject, is given in *The Charities Review*, volume x, pp. 217 ff.

Historical sources, chapters i and ii: Proceedings of New York board of aldermen, board of assistant aldermen, and common council, 1800–1873 (library, city hall), containing reports of superintendent of almshouse and other poor law officials; reports of almshouse commissioner, 1845–1849; reports of board of governors of the almshouse, 1849–1859; reports of commissioners of public charities and correction, 1859–1875. A good résumé is given in "An account of Bellevue hospital, 1736–1893," by R. J. Carlisle (Society of the alumni of Bellevue hospital, New York, 1893). For statement of conditions throughout the state of New York see report on relief and settlement of the poor, by J. V. N. Yates, secretary of state, 1824 (reprinted by the state board of charities, 1900). For sketch of legislation see John Cummings, "Poor laws of Massachusetts and New York" (No. 4, volume x, publications of American economic association, Macmillan, New York, July, 1895). Philadelphia: see report of the committee appointed at a town meeting, etc., July 23, 1827, to consider the pauper system of the city (Philadelphia, 1827); history and reminiscences of the Philadelphia almshouse and the Philadelphia hospital, reprinted from Philadelphia reports (Delve & Blackburn, Philadelphia, 1890); "The picture of Philadelphia," by James Mease, 1811. Boston: see report of commission on the treatment of the poor, by G. S. Hale (Rockwell & Churchill, Boston, 1878). Massachusetts: see reports of state board of charities, 1863–1875. See also centennial proceedings, Charleston orphan house (Charleston, S.C., 1890). Concerning indenture system, see early statutes of the several states.

THE opening of the nineteenth century found the English poor-law system well established in most of the sixteen states then comprising the union. All public charges were cared for by the local administrative units, towns (*i.e.*, townships), counties, or cities, with little or no oversight or control by the states, and, then as now, none by the federal authorities. Adults and children alike, with little distinction, were cared for in one of five ways:

Relief systems affecting destitute children in use at the beginning of the century.

1. By outdoor relief, given to families at their homes.

2. By farming out to a number of families, each pauper being awarded, as a rule, to the lowest bidder.

3. By contract with some individual, usually the lowest bidder, who became responsible for the care of all the paupers of a given locality.

4. By support in an almshouse directly under the control of public authorities.

5. By indenture.

The farming-out and contract systems had comparatively little application so far as children were concerned. Indenture, on the other hand, although especially applicable to children, was, it is curious to note, also used as a means of caring for adults, the statutes of several states providing, at the opening of the century, that idle or vagrant persons might be indentured to respectable citizens for a period of one year.

In tracing the early history of the public care of pauper children it will be necessary to follow for some time the systems of outdoor relief and almshouse care. Outdoor relief was the method by which the larger number of pauper children, as well as adults, were cared for at the beginning of the century. It had already passed (in 1784 in New York) from the control of the church authorities to that of the overseers of the poor. The reports made at a little later date by competent authorities in Boston and New York indicate that public outdoor relief exerted the same evil influences upon children at the opening of the century as it does at the century's close in most of those localities in which it still prevails.

Almshouses were first built by the large cities. Philadelphia, the largest city in the country at the opening of the century (population, 70,287), was then occupying its second public almshouse, opened in 1767 and located in the area bounded by Tenth, Eleventh, Spruce, and Pine streets. Both adults and children were here cared for.

Outdoor relief the predominant method.

Almshouse care confined mostly to the large cities,

New York, the second city in the union (population, 60,489), had just abandoned its original almshouse, and had removed its paupers to a much larger building located in the present city hall park, and on the site of the present county courthouse. Here were numbers of children mingled with the many other elements of almshouse population that in large cities have since been segregated into special classes. The almshouse, while under the immediate management of a superintendent, was controlled by the common council, which held its meetings there and inspected the institution once in three months. On October 6, 1800, a committee of the council, appointed to frame a new set of rules for the management of the almshouse, reported as among the objects to be attained the following:

"The children of the house should be under the government of capable matrons. . . . They should be uniformed, housed, and lodged in separate departments, according to their different sexes; they should be kept as much as possible from the other paupers, habituated to decency, cleanliness, and order, and carefully instructed in reading, writing, and arithmetic. The girls should also be taught to sew and knit.

"When the children arrive at proper ages, great care should be taken to furnish them with suitable places, that they may be instructed in some useful trade or occupation."

The exact number of children in the New York city almshouse in 1801 is not available, but on August 14, 1809, they numbered 226, — 125 boys and 101 girls. It is likely that the city also boarded a number of infants in families at this time. The rules established by the common council in 1800 provided that "Care shall be taken to provide healthy and proper nurses for such of the children as may require them; and where this can be done out of the house, it shall be preferred." Somewhat later, on April 1, 1823, we learn that there were 129 infants placed out "at nurse," and paid for by the city at the rate of $1 per week.

Baltimore, the third city in the union (population, 26,614), probably cared for its destitute children in the Baltimore county almshouse, the city having no charitable institution under its immediate direction at that time.

Boston, the fourth city (population, 24,027), erected its second almshouse, for both children and adults, in 1800. Outdoor relief was also given freely, as was the case very generally throughout New England. The proportion of "unsettled," or state, paupers was increasing, but they were cared for by the cities and towns, which were reimbursed by the state.

There were at this time no other cities in the United States having a population above ten thousand. In most of Pennsylvania, and generally in the southern states, the county system of poor relief prevailed, and many counties had erected almshouses. In Maryland the county almshouse system was established by law in 1768. In Delaware each county had an almshouse by 1823.

but county almshouses in rural districts also common in the south.

So far as known, the only public institution for children, not forming part of an almshouse, existing in 1801 was the Charleston, S.C., orphan house. The charter of Charleston, granted at the close of the revolutionary war, imposed upon the city the duty of providing for poor orphans. For some years the children were boarded in families, but in 1790 a resolution was adopted by the city council in favor of the establishment of an orphan house. At first a building was hired for this purpose, but a structure erected by the city was opened October 18, 1794, to receive the 115 orphans who were city charges. The records of the institution tell

Only one public institution expressly for children then on record.

of an appreciative visit to it by President
Washington.

The plan of indenturing or apprenticing
destitute children, also taken from the English poor law, was in very general use at the
opening of the century. It had been carefully regulated by law in Massachusetts in
1703, in New York in 1754, in Pennsylvania in 1771, and in Maryland in 1797, and
doubtless found legal recognition in still
earlier statutes in these and other states. The
rules established by the common council for
the government of the New York almshouse
in 1800 provided that "When any of the
children arrive at proper ages they shall be
bound out to suitable trades or occupations,
and provision shall be made in their indenture
for their due maintenance and instruction. If
any of those who shall have been so bound
out shall be injured or ill-treated, the superintendent shall consider it as his duty to procure them redress. They are to be considered
in every respect as the children of the public,
under his care." In Virginia overseers of
the poor were required by law to make
monthly reports, to the county courts, of the
poor orphans and other children bound out.

The eighteenth century had seen the beginnings of a remarkable development of pri-

*Indenture
in general
use.*

vate charities for the care of children. The first orphan asylum in the country was that attached to the Ursuline convent in New Orleans. This convent was established in 1727, under the auspices of Louis XV of France. It maintained a day school and a hospital, and also received, during the first year, an orphan rescued by a missionary from a dissolute family. The frightful massacre by the Natchez Indians in 1729 left many orphans in and near New Orleans, and the convent established an asylum for their care. In 1824 the convent was removed to a country site, and owing to the growth of other asylums provision was made for the care of but thirty orphans, which number the convent still maintains.

A few private charities for children had been established.

The Bethesda orphan house was established in Savannah in 1738, five years after the colony was settled, by the celebrated preacher, George Whitefield, to whom, he states, the plan was suggested by Charles Wesley and Governor Oglethorpe. This was founded by funds collected by Whitefield in England. In 1797 the society for the relief of poor widows with small children was organized in New York city. This society did not establish an institution, but visited and gave relief to widows and children in their homes, — a beneficent work which it continues to the present. In 1798 an association was organized by a Roman catholic priest in Philadelphia to care for the orphans of catholics who died of yellow fever during that year. Subsequently this institution became St. Joseph's female orphan asylum. In 1799 an asylum for the care and education of destitute girls was established by St. Paul's church in Baltimore, and in 1800 the Boston female asylum for indigent orphan girls was incorporated.

As to destitute children, the situation at the opening of the century may be summed up in the statement that children who were public charges were, as a rule, cared for with adult paupers by the contract system, or in almshouses, or by outdoor relief, or were bound out as apprentices; that Charleston had a municipal orphan asylum; and that private institutions for children had been established in New Orleans, Savannah, New York, Philadelphia, Baltimore, and Boston.

As to neglected children, we find in the statutes of the time but few provisions for their rescue and care. As early as 1735 in Boston children whose parents were unable or neglected to provide for their support and education might be bound out by the overseers of the poor. The laws of Maryland

Neglected children practically overlooked.

authorized in 1797 the binding out of the children of beggars. The class of children who are now forcibly removed from the control of unfit parents apparently remained with their families, as a rule, until the latter became destitute, when the children were cared for as pauper children, or until the fruits of neglect were reaped, and the children, convicted of offences, were sent to jails and penitentiaries along with older offenders. In the penitentiary of New York city, on April 1, 1823, we are informed, there were thirty-two boys.

CHAPTER II

PUBLIC CARE OF DESTITUTE CHILDREN,
1801–1875

AGENCIES for the care of destitute children have sprung from two sources, — from public bodies acting in behalf of the whole community, and from private benevolence exercised through individual or associated effort. The
Public care defined. term public, as used throughout this volume in connection with institutions or agencies for the care of children, indicates such as are under the direct control of governmental bodies and are supported from public funds. The term private indicates all other agencies, whether managed by individuals or by societies, churches, or corporations.

The public care of children during the first three quarters of the century follows, in the main, the changes in the care of adult paupers, though in the larger cities provision was made
Its evolution mainly through the almshouse. for them separate from the adults, but under the same administrative control. The movement as a whole was toward an increased use of almshouses and a relative diminution of

12

outdoor relief. The farming-out and contract systems passed largely into disuse, and in some states were forbidden by law.

As it is fairly indicative of the manner in which most municipal institutions for children have been conducted, the history of the care of children by the city of New York will be considered at some length. That of other important municipalities will follow more briefly. The typical experience of New York city.

The common council of New York, whose minutes during the first three quarters of the century afford many illustrations of aldermanic wisdom as applied to child-saving, appointed January 7, 1805, a committee to consider and report upon the expediency of granting the application of the commissioners of the almshouse for the establishment at the almshouse of a school for the pauper children. Whether the school was established or not we do not know. In 1816 the children were removed, with the almshouse paupers, the hospital, and the prison department, to the new Bellevue establishment at Twenty-sixth street and East river, — the main building of which is now used as Bellevue hospital. On April 1, 1823, there were 553 children in the Bellevue almshouse, and the number of children in families aided by public outdoor The Bellevue establishment.

relief was estimated at 4000. Here, at least, a school was provided, for a writer in 1826 describing the almshouse establishment says, "One of the public or free schools (No. 6), conducted upon the monitorial system and containing 300 scholars, is in appropriate rooms for males and females. The school is well conducted, and the teachers are under the direction of the public school committee of the city. The children are orderly, clean, decently clothed, and in good health," — an optimistic report, not altogether sustained by later developments. The writer continues, "There are two brick buildings, one at each end of the factory, seventy-five by twenty-five feet, containing six rooms each, which were formerly occupied as hospitals, one for men and one for women, who have been removed to the new hospital, and these rooms are now used for children and their nurses." The almshouse census in 1828 showed that the number of juvenile inmates had increased during the preceding five years from 553 to 667.

A severe outbreak of ophthalmia in 1831 proved to be the beginning of the end of the use of the Bellevue establishment as a home for pauper children. On May 23, 1831, the board of assistant aldermen directed the committee on charity and the almshouse to report at the next meeting the present condition of the almshouse children afflicted with ophthalmia, and the cause. A month later the common council authorized the committee to employ a physician to assist the resident physician in the treatment of these children. He was to receive $3 for each day on which he visited them.

Just at this time the city purchased Blackwell's island, and also three farms in Queens county, located on the East river opposite Blackwell's island and known as the Long Island farms. A portion of the children having ophthalmia were removed from Bellevue to the island. In July, the commissioners of the almshouse were authorized to remove the convalescent children from here to the Long Island farms, and to transfer from the almshouse to Blackwell's island the residue of the children afflicted with ophthalmia. On July 22, 1831, a committee of the board of assistant aldermen reported that they had visited the children on the island, and found that "their general health was manifestly changed from a sickly hue to a robust appearance."

A little later, on December 5, 1831, we find the following resolution adopted by the

Ravages of ophthalmia call public attention to the condition of children in the almshouse,

assistant aldermen : "Whereas, several of the
children at the Alms House having been
afflicted by the disease termed Ophtalma,
therefore, Resolved, that it be referred to
the Committee of the Alms House to ascertain and report to this Board whether they
can be taught any and what useful employ-
ments that may render them less burthen-
some to themselves, and what will be the
probable expense."

In June, 1832, the common council received a communication from the almshouse
commissioners, recommending that the children in that establishment be transferred to
the Long Island farms, stating that it would
be necessary to erect temporary buildings at
each of the three farms, and stating also that
120 of the almshouse children had ophthalmia. This recommendation was acted upon,
for one of the commissioners, in a letter of
resignation dated July 1, 1833, stated that
most of the children had been transferred
from Bellevue to the Long Island farms,
which were originally intended "for the
special benefit of this unoffending, interesting, and numerous class of paupers." The
commissioner goes on to state that "soon
after the purchase of the farms, in 1831, a
man was placed upon them, ostensibly to cut

and they
were re-
moved to
Long
Island,

wood in winter, his large family to be supported, and he to have $2 per day besides."
The commissioner complains that, although
the man is not qualified to superintend either
the farms or the children, he still remains
in charge of both. As a consequence, he
says, "118 boys dined last Saturday upon
dry, hard, boiled salt beef, with dry bread,
but no vegetables." He closes: "I would
anxiously but respectfully recommend to your
honorable bodies that you do consider the
case of these poor children." From this
time all of the children, except perhaps those
needing hospital care, and the infants who
were boarded out, were kept at the Long
Island farms. On September 1, 1834, they
numbered 680, and 130 were at nurse in the
city. The numbers increased, for the commissioners at this time announced the policy
of "readily receiving all children who belong
to the city and are destitute, and when once
within the establishment keeping them under
all usual circumstances until they are taught
to read and write." They adopted a rule that
girls should not be bound out under the age
of ten years, nor boys under the age of
twelve, stating that during the previous year
eighty children under those ages had been
indentured. A question that is still trouble-

where all destitute children of the city were freely received.

some to all institutions caring for children was thus stated in the report of the almshouse commissioners for 1834:

"The commissioners can bind the children out the day they enter the almshouse, and the parents lose all control over them; but if they remain in the almshouse unbound, the parents or guardians can probably demand them and take them out. Now if they are once abandoned by their parents or friends to the public, and put in the almshouse school, it should be optional with the commissioners to deliver them back to the parents and friends or not. It will be readily perceived that there are many cases in which the taking of the children from school and delivering them back to intemperate parents, perhaps criminal ones, would be the certain destruction of the little education obtained, and to the welfare and morals of the children." The report goes on to state that the Long Island farms are, to a considerable extent, in an uncultivated state, but that they believe the citizens will not regret the purchase when they consider "that the previous abode of these children was within high walls, containing a state prison, county prison, a bridewell, and an almshouse establishment."

Almost immediately, however, an agitation

The difficulty of retaining these children till fairly schooled.

was begun for the sale of the Long Island farms and the removal of the children to Randall's island, which was purchased by the city in 1835. In the same year a committee of the board of aldermen reported in favor of moving both the children's institutions and the almshouse to Randall's island. Nothing was effected for some years, although the subject was reported upon nearly every year.

The Long Island establishment proving unsatisfactory,

The message of the mayor, May, 1840, states that there were 900 children in the schools on the Long Island farms, and that 349 children had been bound out during the preceding year. In 1843 plans were adopted by the almshouse commissioners for the removal of both the almshouse and the children's institutions to Blackwell's island. Buildings were to be erected just north of the present site of the almshouse, to accommodate 1000 children. This plan was not carried into effect, and in 1845 the Long Island farms had been sold, and a large building was erected on Randall's island for the pauper children. This, however, burned before the children were removed to it, and the question again arose as to where they should be located. It was finally decided to erect a series of detached buildings on Randall's island. Early in 1847 the large building

after much delay and a brief sojourn with the adult paupers on Blackwell's island,

now occupied by the almshouse for women
on Blackwell's island was completed, and the
children were removed thither, "owing to the
dilapidation of the old and wretched Long
Island farms hovels." Here they remained
a year, during which time ten brick buildings
were erected for them on Randall's island.
The commissioner again stated it to be his
intention to retain the children, before indenturing them, until they had received a
better education. He thought girls should
not leave the institution until they were thirteen years, and boys, fifteen years of age.
He also condemned unsparingly the custom
of detailing adult paupers, vagrants, and even
criminals from the city institutions to care for
the children. "Proper and efficient nurses
should be hired, whose characters are a guarantee for the propriety of their actions." On
April 15, 1848, the children were removed to
the Randall's island institutions, and the commissioner triumphantly reported, "We can
certainly now, after having been incommoded
with miserable and unsightly hovels for many
years, boast with a becoming pride of possess-
ing the most complete, convenient, and ele-
gant establishment for the rearing of young
orphans of the city's care known in the
world; — here true humanity can fulfill its

the chil-
dren were
removed to
Randall's
island,
1848.

ennobling mission." There remained in the Randall's island institutions, December 31, 1848, a total of 1054 children. There were also 165 children at nurse. During 1849, 514 children were cared for at nurse; of them fifty were adopted, ninety-seven were restored to friends, and 280 died. This was a cholera year, and, commenting on the death rate, the clerk of the outdoor poor department remarks that "The mortality among the children at nurse for the almshouse was awfully fatal and extensive." Of the 109 children boarded out at the close of 1849, "about thirty-six" were reported as illegitimate children, mostly boarded with their mothers, twenty-seven as foundlings, and forty-six as the children of destitute parents. At this time the almshouse was under the control of one commissioner. Among other improvements, he employed an agent to visit the children at nurse, and also those indentured. The report for 1848 contains interesting statements concerning many of the children visited, thus, — "Bridget ——, with Michael ——, 349 Water St., about seven years; is now fourteen years old; a very industrious girl; reads, writes, and ciphers." "Mary ——, with William ——, on 27th St., for two and one half years; is now fourteen

Children boarded out at nurse.

years old; education neglected, — promised to attend to it." " James ——, with ——, 205 Christie St., for two years and one half; is nine years old; a very good boy."

In 1849 a board of governors succeeded the almshouse commissioner, and to some extent reversed his policy. They were in favor

of placing children in families, and believed that legislation should be had enabling them to indenture children in other states. They stated that, while they had been able to supply most of the demand for indenturing, no girls "capable of being put out remained," although there were still a number of boys of suitable age and size.

From 1849 the history of the Randall's island nurseries is uneventful, until the legis-

lation of 1875, which forbade the city to retain in its institutions healthy children over two years of age. The early reports of the state board of charities and of the state charities aid association contain many unsparing criticisms of the pitiful condition of the children, cared for in part by female prisoners from the workhouse.

The boarding out of infants continued until some date between 1863 and 1866, when they were all returned to the almshouse. In 1866 an infant's department of the almshouse was created, where, the report states, the "foundling infants, hitherto distributed among the wards of the almshouse, and consigned to the mercies of reluctant attendants, have been gathered under the care of a matron and kind and attentive nurses." This was at first called the infants' bureau, and in 1867 the erection of a large new building for its use on Randall's island was begun. During the winter of 1867–8, owing to the overcrowding of the almshouse, the infants' hospital was removed to the newly erected building intended for an inebriate asylum, where it remained until August, 1869, when it was removed to its present building on Randall's island. The death rate continued high, however, and the boarding out in Westchester county of the foundling and motherless babies was begun in 1871 or 1872. Boarding out was discontinued in 1890, but was renewed on a small scale in 1898, with the coöperation of two private charities. It was so successful in reducing the death rate that in 1900 and 1901 it was extended to include all foundlings coming directly under the care of the city of New York.

Varying policy regarding infants.

Philadelphia continued to occupy the almshouse located at Tenth and Pine streets until about 1835. In 1810 the average number of

Philadelphia's experience.

children supported in the institution was 171, and during the same year an average of 212 children were supported "at nurse out of the house."

In 1820, a long time before New York or Boston made separate provision for pauper children, the almshouse managers established a children's asylum, on Fifth street near Pine, and we are told by a writer in 1830 that "The good effects of this change upon the health and morals of the children are very perceptible." The rules and regulations for the internal government of the almshouse, adopted December 21, 1821, contain elaborate provisions in regard to the children in the asylum, and particularly in regard to the conduct of the school in the institution. Among other interesting provisions are the following: "The teacher shall use lenity and kindness to the boys under his care, and in no case inflict corporal punishment. . . . The punishment for bad behavior shall be bread and water, and solitary confinement, if necessary, for an hour or two. . . . The books recommended are Pierce's 'Spelling book,' Mrs. Barbauld's 'Easy lessons,' and the New Testament. . . . It shall be the duty of the teacher to attend with his scholars at divine service when in the house, and keep them as

Children separated from pauper adults, 1820.

much as possible silent and in order, and place them by themselves."

The report of a committee appointed at a town meeting of the citizens of the city and county of Philadelphia, July 23, 1827, to consider the subject of the pauper system of the city and districts, and to report remedies for its defects, throws much light on the operations of the children's asylum. The number of children admitted from the opening of the asylum in April, 1820, to May 22, 1826, was, boys 661, girls 328, total 989. The disposition made of them was as follows:

Statistics of the children's asylum.

	Boys	Girls	Total
Bound out	110	72	182
Died	34	17	51
Discharged	29	16	45
Eloped	25	4	29
Returned to parents and relatives . .	334	188	522
Out on trial, 1826	11	4	15
In the asylum, 1826 . . .	118	27	145
	661	328	989

The average age of those admitted had been about four and one half years; the average stay in the asylum of those who were returned to parents and relatives was little over six months, and of those who ran away about three months; the average age of those bound out had been seven years, and they had been in the asylum an average of two years and four months. The average number in the asylum during the preceding year was 154, and the average per capita cost per week 91¼ cents. The total cost of the asylum from 1820 to 1826, not including cost of house, lot, and a new additional building, had been $44,508. In addition to the children in the asylum, there remained in the almshouse proper, on September 1, 1827, only fourteen children under five years of age, three between five and ten, and sixteen between ten and twenty. There were also thirteen children under ten in the almshouse infirmary.

Among the defects enumerated by the committee was the lack of authority in the board of guardians to bind out children who became public charges, without the consent of the parents. The report stated, "The children of paupers are received into the asylum, nursed when necessary, fed and comfortably clothed at a very great expense to the public; as soon as they arrive at a suitable age to be bound out and proper places are provided for them, they are frequently with-

Children withdrawn by parents too easily.

drawn by their parents and return to the haunts of poverty and vice from which they had been taken, and thus the benevolent purposes of the institution are defeated and the public funds uselessly expended." The committee recommended that the buildings occupied as an almshouse and children's asylum be sold and new buildings erected; that "the children's asylum be so constructed as to guard against the diseases to which the inmates of the present establishment are subject," and that the board of guardians be given power to bind out children who become public charges without the consent of parents, unless the expenses incurred for their support be defrayed and a security be given that they will not again become chargeable for two years.

The recommendation of the committee as to the sale of the buildings was carried into effect, but unfortunately the lesson learned fifteen years earlier was forgotten and, just as New York was beginning to separate her children from adult paupers, Philadelphia took a backward step, and brought her children under the same roof with the adults. In 1835 the children's asylum and the almshouse were sold, and both children and adults were removed to the new buildings located in

The separate children's asylum sold, and children again mingled with adult paupers, 1835.

the town of Blockley (now part of Philadelphia), and known henceforth as the Blockley almshouse. The children were placed in the east end of the northwestern range of buildings.

From Dr. Alfred Stillé's reminiscences of the Philadelphia hospital we learn something of the condition of the children in this institution. Dr. Stillé was a resident physician of the institution in its earliest days, and had special charge of the children's asylum. He says, " A hundred or more children were sheltered there on their way to the early grave to which most of them were destined. Illegitimate and other outcasts formed the majority, and ophthalmia, that curse of children's asylums, made of them a sore-eyed, puny group most pitiable to see. I soon became convinced of the causes that produced the crippling and mortality of these outcasts and waifs. I pointed out to the committee of the board how the disease was disseminated by the children washing in the same basins and using the same towels, and, it was maintained, by their having no shady places for exercise in the open air, and also by the insufficient food permitted them. . . . But, of course, the committee of the children's asylum and the guardians knew better than I, and, at the

Conditions at the Blockley almshouse,

time at least, nothing was done to correct this wrong."

where dependent children continued to be housed until 1883.

So far as we can ascertain, the destitute children supported by the city of Philadelphia remained in Blockley almshouse until the passage of the children's law of 1883, a period of forty-eight years.

The city of Boston, which had built an almshouse in 1800, soon found it outgrown, and in 1822 a new structure was completed in South Boston, known as the house of industry. This institution (both almshouse and prison, and receiving both children and adults) was placed under the charge of a body called the board of directors of the house of industry. Controversy arising between this body and the overseers of the poor, the functions of the overseers were by statute limited to the distribution of outdoor relief, and of certain trust funds. The custody of the pauper children of the almshouse was vested henceforth in the directors of the house of industry. Although the city established a reform school for juvenile offenders in 1826 (located, unfortunately, in a portion of the buildings of the house of correction for adult offenders), no separate provision for pauper children was made until much later. The need of removing the children from adult paupers was, how-

Boston.

Juvenile reformatory established, 1826.

ever, realized by the directors of the house of industry, for in 1833 their annual report states that "In closing these remarks the directors would respectfully urge the necessity of removing the children from the adult paupers. Experience has shown that children brought up and indented from almshouses often feel toward it a filial regard, and having been accustomed to see grown persons supported there for no other reason than that they are addicted to idleness and intemperance, again resort to it themselves rather than encounter the common difficulties of life." The report for 1834 speaks of ten children at the almshouse likely to remain permanent paupers (on account of idiocy, etc.), and 122 who will probably be indentured as they arrive at a suitable age, or be discharged to parents and friends. In the same year, 1834, the city council established at the house of industry a building known as the "children's asylum." The overseers of the poor appropriated the income from one of the principal trust funds under their care, the Boylston education fund, to the support of certain children in this institution, which henceforth was known as the Boylston school, or Boylston asylum, though remaining a part of the house of industry.

Dependent children partly separated from adult paupers, 1834.

In 1837 the house of reformation (juvenile reformatory) was transferred to a building erected, against the protest of the managers, near the house of correction and house of industry. It was at this time under a control separate from that of any other institution, but in 1841 the city council made it a part of the house of industry, placing it under the control of the board of directors of the latter institution. The destitute boys who had been in the Boylston school or asylum were transferred to a wing of the house of reformation building, and placed under the officers of the latter institution, though they were kept "quite separate." Provision was thus made for a portion of the pauper children somewhat apart from the adult paupers and criminals, but in the same building with juvenile offenders.

Juvenile delinquents and dependents brought together, 1841.

In 1849 a large building was erected on Deer island, and thither were removed the inmates of the house of industry, — adult prisoners, adult paupers, and juvenile paupers, except the boys over six years of age who remained in one wing of the house of reformation for juvenile offenders in South Boston. This institution also was removed to Deer island in 1858. Presumably the pauper children were in separate buildings

Deer island, 1849, — adults and children practically in one institution.

on Deer island, for the report of 1853 speaks of two schools on Deer island, in one of which were seventy girls and small boys, and in the other 116 older boys. There were also 131 boys in the Boylston school, or juvenile pauper wing of the house of reformation building, making a total of 317 indoor juvenile paupers. The next year, 1854, 214 children were reported at Deer island, and fifty-nine " at nurse."

No further radical changes occurred until after 1875. At the close of the first three quarters of the century Boston provided for its destitute and neglected children in buildings on Deer island which were under the control of the almshouse authorities, and practically formed a part of that institution.

The history of the Charleston orphan house, a strictly municipal institution, from 1790 to the present, has been in every way creditable to that city. The institution still stands on the site of the original building erected in 1794. It has received a number of bequests and donations from private citizens, so that about half of its present income is derived from this source, and half from the city treasury. The first kindergarten in Charleston was established at the orphan house in 1877. The government of the

Charleston's orphan house, the single exception to the general failure of municipal care of destitute children.

institution is vested in ten commissioners appointed by the city council.

Notwithstanding the success of the Charleston orphan house, few persons, if any, will dissent from the statement that the direct care of destitute children by American municipalities prior to 1875 was, as a rule, a pitiful failure.

In the meantime, the state of Massachusetts, which since about 1793 had reimbursed the various towns and cities for the care of the "unsettled poor," had made its own provision for this class by establishing, in 1851–2, three state almshouses, at Tewksbury, Bridgewater, and Monson. At each of these, children, as well as adults, were received. In 1855 an act was passed requiring the removal of all children from Bridgewater and Tewksbury to Monson, but through the influence of the superintendents of the three institutions it was repealed the next year. By 1858 the population of these three institutions exceeded 2500, of whom more than half were children. This population was described by the board of state charities as "a motley collection of broken-backed, lame-legged, sore-eyed, helpless, and infirm human beings, with scarcely an adult that is able in body and mind." We are informed

State care in Massachusetts.

that the children were packed like sardines in double cradles ; were cared for by pauper inmates, and were indentured to people whose credentials could hardly have received a proper investigation at the hands of the overworked house officials. The board of state charities, established in 1863, was authorized to transfer inmates of any state almshouse to any other state almshouse. One of its first acts, in 1864, was to transfer the children from Bridgewater and Tewksbury to Monson. Subsequently, in 1866, the Monson institution was declared to be the state primary school, and thereafter the children were not to be designated as paupers. This was the first state institution for destitute children in the United States. In 1872 the almshouse department at Monson was abolished, though many adult paupers remained in the state primary school as helpers.

Transfer of state children to Monson, 1864, and designation of this institution as the " state primary school."

The board of state charities engaged an agent to visit the children who had been indentured from the state almshouses and the state reform schools. This led to the establishment, in 1869, of a state visiting agency, to visit all children placed out from state institutions, and to visit and report upon the homes of applicants for children. The visiting agency was independent of any other

Establishment of state visiting agency, 1869.

state body, its executive officer being appointed by the governor, but it reported to the board of state charities. It was also the duty of the visiting agent to attend trials of juvenile offenders, and, having investigated the circumstances, to advise the magistrates whether the children should be committed to a reform school, or to the custody of the board of state charities, to be placed by it with their parents or in other families, or temporarily in the state primary school at Monson, later on to be placed in families, or if they proved unmanageable, transferred to reform schools. Thus early were the essential features of flexibility and transfer from one institution to another, or to a family, according to the developments of the individual child, secured. By 1875, Massachusetts, so far as its state charges were concerned, had separated its juvenile from its adult paupers, and had established an adequate system of supervision of indentured children.

Flexibility in disposition of children secured.

Meanwhile, almshouses had been established by many smaller cities, and in some states by counties or towns. Perhaps the most complete statement of the methods of public care of the poor in the earlier part of the century is contained in the report of

Experience in New York state.

an investigation made by the then secretary of the state of New York, Hon. J. V. N. Yates, in 1823. This report includes not only a statement of the condition of the poor in each county and town in New York, but also a detailed report from nearly every other state in the union. The report from Brooklyn showed that there were thirteen boys and seven girls in the almshouse, and also thirteen men and twenty-one women. The training received by the children is perhaps suggested by the report of the Brooklyn official: "It is indispensable that the children should be educated, but in some almshouses (as it is in ours at present) there may be none able to teach the children ; and on account of disorders incident to public places, it would be improper to send them to the public district school; the children must remain uneducated or some provision must be made to hire a teacher. Would it not be right to give the almshouse a particular demand on the school fund ?" In Albany, of 126 paupers in the almshouse in 1823, forty-six were children under the age of seven years.

The Yates report, 1823.

The general conclusion reached by Mr. Yates was that outdoor relief was harmful, and that the building of county almshouses would solve most of the difficulties connected with public relief. The report stated that "The education and morals of the children of paupers (except in almshouses) are almost wholly neglected. They grow up in filth, idleness, and disease, and many become early candidates for the prison or the grave. The evidence on this head is too voluminous for reference."

Again, in summing up the situation, the report states: "Most of the children of paupers out of an almshouse are not only brought up in ignorance and idleness, but their health is precarious, and they frequently die prematurely. The reverse is the case in an almshouse. Their health and morals are alike improved and secured, and besides they receive an education to fit them for future usefulness."

It was recommended that in every county there should be established one or more houses of employment, in which paupers were to be maintained and employed, and their children to be carefully instructed, and at suitable ages to be put out to some useful business or trade.

The report received favorable consideration, and led to the passage of the law of 1824, which established the county almshouse system in New York.

County almshouses encouraged, as affording opportunity to educate pauper children.

The rapidly developing central and western states generally adopted systems of poor relief similar to those of New York and Pennsylvania, though the contract and farming-out plans seem to have found small place in those states. The town overseers generally were authorized to give temporary outdoor relief, but permanent outdoor relief, if given, and the almshouses, were administered by the county authorities.

It gradually became evident to thoughtful observers that the high hopes of Secretary Yates, expressed in his report of 1824, that in almshouses the children of paupers would be trained and taught to be useful, and thus become desirable members of society, were not to be fulfilled. Miss Dorothea Lynde Dix, in her report of her visitation of the almshouses of New York in 1844, said: "They do not guard against the indiscriminate association of the children with the adult poor. The education of these children, with rare exceptions, is conducted on a very defective plan. The almshouse schools, so far as I have learned from frequent inquiries, are not inspected by official persons, who visit and examine the other schools of the county."

Experience, however, condemned almshouse shelter of children.

In 1856 a select committee appointed by the New York senate made a careful report on the public charities of the state. The condition of the almshouses generally was unsparingly condemned, and especially their harmful effects upon the children. "The committee are forced to say that it is a great public reproach that they [the children] should be permitted to remain in the poorhouses. As they are now mismanaged, they are for the young the worst possible nurseries." From this time on, the conviction slowly spread that poorhouses were not good places for children to grow up in. In the fulness of time, almost twenty years after the above report was submitted by the senate committee, legislation began to be secured prohibiting the retention of children in almshouses.

The indenture system was a very important part of the provision for destitute children during the first three quarters of the century. The statutes of many states contained elaborate provisions with regard to the indenturing of children. Some of these are interesting. The Massachusetts act of 1793 directed that in indentures "Provision shall be made for instructing the male children to read, write, and cipher," and "For such other instruction, benefit, and allowance either within or at the end of the term, as to the overseers may seem fit and reasonable," — a

Indenture in general use for many years,

degree of flexibility and adaptiveness to individual cases that has sometimes been lacking
in more modern legislation. In Maryland in
1793 an act was passed "For the better regulation of apprentices," indicating that there
had been earlier legislation upon the subject.
The preamble recited, "Whereas, it has been
found by experience that poor children,
orphans, and illegitimate, for want of some
efficient system have been left destitute of
support and have become useless or depraved
members of society; And, Whereas it would
greatly conduce to the good of the public in
general and of such children in particular that
necessary instruction in trades and useful arts
should be afforded them; Therefore," etc.
The justices of the orphans' courts were
authorized to bind out orphans, "and such
children as are suffering through the extreme
indigence or poverty of their parents, also the
children of beggars, and also illegitimate children, and the children of persons out of this
state where a sufficient sustenance is not
afforded." Trustees of the poor in the various counties were authorized to bind out children under their care in the poorhouses,
preferably to tradesmen and mechanics. In
1826 the act was amended so as to authorize the binding out of children who were

found begging upon the streets of the city
of Baltimore. The indenture system was
authorized by law in the territory of Indiana
in 1807. The annual message of the mayor
of the city of New York for the year 1840
states that 349 children had been bound out
during the preceding year.

The old-fashioned indenture or apprentice
system passed largely into disuse, if not into
disrepute, by 1875. It is clearly not in har-
mony with the spirit of these later times to
"bind" any one to serve another person for a
definite term of years. The bound child has
often been alluded to as typifying loneliness,
neglect, overwork, and a consciousness of be-
ing held in low esteem. *but aban-doned toward the latter part of the century,*

It is probable, however, that in the earlier
part of the century the system was not without merit, and that as the apprentice system
as a whole passed away with the profound
changes that occurred in industrial conditions,
the indenturing of children underwent a
change for the worse. The value of the
instruction received from the "masters" became less, and the value of the services rendered by the children increased. In its worst
forms, and especially in some localities, certain features of the indenture system, particu-
larly the recapture of apprentices who ran *as chang-ing indus-trial conditions made the relation of apprentice to master less inti-mate and kindly.*

away, painfully remind one of human slavery. In fact, it has been seriously suggested that by the adoption of the constitutional amendment, in 1865, forbidding "involuntary servitude," the indenture system became unconstitutional. In the early part of the century, however, when learning a trade was a matter of the highest importance, the system was undoubtedly something quite different from what it became in later years. Though there were doubtless many cases of hardship from exacting or cruel masters, it is likely that the indentured children, as a whole, were more fortunate than those maintained by public outdoor relief or in almshouses. Miss Mary E. Wilkins, in a collection of stories for children, tells a pretty story of a bound girl who was afterwards adopted, and gives an authentic copy of an indenture paper executed in Boston in 1753.[1]

[1] "The pot of gold," Lothrop, Boston, 1893.

CHAPTER III

PRIVATE CHARITIES FOR DESTITUTE CHILDREN, 1801–1875

Historical sources : Minutes of union society, Savannah, 1750–1858, with historical sketch of Bethesda orphan asylum (J. M. Cooper & Co., Savannah, 1860) ; also proceedings of the 114th anniversary of the union society, April 25, 1899. Reprint of annual reports of the orphan asylum society of New York city, 1806–1896 (2 vols., published by the society). For sketch of several endowed institutions see L. P. Alden's article in report of committee on history of child-saving, national conference of charities and correction, 1893 ; also article by W. P. Letchworth in same volume. The reports of Girard college are included in the reports of the board of city trusts, Philadelphia. " The dangerous classes of New York," by C. L. Brace (Wynkoop & Hallenbeck, New York, 1872), gives views and experiences of the founder of the children's aid society. See also early reports of the New York children's aid society. For early history of many New York private institutions see " The charities of New York, Brooklyn, and Staten Island," by H. J. Cammann and H. N. Camp (Hurd & Houghton, New York, 1868) ; and "New York and its institutions, 1604–1872," by J. F. Richmond (Treat, New York, 1872). Scharf & Westcott's history of Philadelphia, volume ii, has a chapter on Philadelphia charities. " The memorial history of Boston," 1881, has a chapter by G. S. Hale on the charities of Boston. Report of Boston (female) orphan asylum for 1898 includes historical statement. Reports of Boston asylum and farm school for indigent boys. Acts of incorporation, by-laws, etc., of Baltimore orphan asylum, 1891. See early reports of the New York catholic protec-

43

tory, 1863–1875, and of the New York juvenile asylum, 1851–1875. "Catholic child-helping agencies in the United States," national conference of charities and correction, 1896; Jewish child-saving in the United States, national conference of charities and correction, 1897. See also reports Massachusetts infant asylum, 1867–1875; nursery and child's hospital, New York, 1854–1875; and Boston children's aid society, 1863–1875.

THOUGH there has been throughout the century a steady growth in the number and importance of children's institutions founded from philanthropic motives and supported by the gifts of the generous, it seems best to divide their history into two chapters,— 1801 to 1875, and 1875 to the close of the century. The establishment of public systems of child-saving work in various states in the decade 1870–1880, and the enactment of laws for the removal of children from almshouses, changed the conditions under which the private charities did their work, and in some states strongly affected their character and methods. The work of the private agencies for the care of destitute children after 1875 will therefore be taken up after we have considered the public systems adopted in various states in place of caring for children in almshouses.

Prior to the opening of the nineteenth century agencies for the care of destitute children had been established by private benevolence in the cities of New Orleans, Savannah, New York, Philadelphia, Baltimore, and Boston. The orphan asylum founded by Whitefield in Savannah in 1738 passed through many vicissitudes, and gradually became an academy rather than an orphan home. It was Whitefield's wish to have it become a college, but his majesty, George II, declined to grant a college charter. The buildings were twice burned, and the academy was closed in 1791. The five other organizations founded prior to 1801 have continued their work to the present.

The first private charities for children.

The first charity for children organized in the United States after 1800 was the New York orphan asylum society. During the early days of the society for the relief of widows with small children, organized in 1797, the question often arose as to how the children of deceased widows should be cared for, the funds of the society not being available for their support. A copy of the life of Francke, with a history of his orphan house at Halle, fell into the hands of one of the managers of the society, and this led to the establishment of the orphan asylum society.

New York orphan asylum society, 1806.

The original constitution of the society, adopted in 1807, provided that admittance should be granted only to orphans, who should be educated, fed, and clothed at the expense of the society, and at the asylum. It was further provided that, "As soon as the age and acquirements of orphans shall, in the opinion of the board of direction, render them capable of earning their living they must be bound out to some reputable persons or families for such object and in such manner as the board shall approve."

Its policy: rudimentary education, followed by indenture.

In the absence of a public school system it was natural that the managers should feel that the admission of the children was necessary for their education, no less than for their maintenance. It would have been very difficult at that time to secure the education of children placed out in free homes or boarded in families. The early reports of the society all indicate that the children were to be placed out as soon as they had received a fair education. The by-laws provided that, "The boys shall be bound to farmers or mechanics, the girls to respectable families. A book shall be kept at the asylum in which applicants for children shall insert their names, occupations, and references for character, which shall be laid before the board. At the monthly meeting a committee shall be appointed to make the necessary inquiries." In the charter of the society, granted by the legislature in 1807, its purposes were declared to be "protecting, relieving, and instructing orphan children."

The third annual report states that the plan of the society is, "To bind out the girls as servants from the time they can read and write until they are eighteen; and the boys, when equally instructed, are to be put out as servants till the age of fifteen, at which time they are to be returned to the trustees of the asylum, who will then bind them as apprentices to virtuous mechanics."

Before the society was two years old, finding itself encumbered with debt, it applied to the state legislature for assistance, an unfortunate example that has been very generally followed by New York children's institutions. The legislature responded by extending the grant of a lottery which it had previously made to the board of health, upon condition that $5000 of the proceeds should be paid to the orphan asylum society. The sum of $5000 was received from the proceeds of this lottery in 1815, but meanwhile, in 1811, the legislature granted the society an annual contribution of $500, to be paid from the duties on auction sales, a sum which the society received each year until 1853.

Appeal to the public treasury for a subsidy.

The early reports of the society indicate that a considerable number of their children were received directly from the almshouse. The society often stated with pride, that no orphan child had ever been refused admission to the institution. The twelfth report states that in the month of February eleven orphan children were received from the New York almshouse, and adds that " The honorable, the corporation, have never been prevailed upon to extend even a small share of that patronage to this society which it might seem to claim from them, and for which they had been repeatedly solicited." An interesting glimpse of the life of the children in the asylum is afforded by the fourteenth annual report, which informs us that " The boys have been employed in reading, writing, arithmetic, and committing scripture to memory, thirty-four boys having learned from 150 to 1500 verses each, and one has committed the whole of the New Testament. For health and recreation they have, under the direction of the superintendent, cultivated the ground owned or rented by the society."

Occupations of the children.

The sixteenth annual report, dated April, 1822, stated that since the commencement of the society there had been received 446

children, of whom 243 had been placed
with respectable employers, a number were
out on trial, fifteen had died, and 152
remained in the asylum.

A year after the New York orphan asylum
was organized, a society in Baltimore, known
as the female orphaline charity school, pur- Baltimore
chased a house and added to its educational orphan
work the care and maintenance of desti- asylum,
tute children. It had been established
in 1778 as the female humane associated
charity school. Although the care of children was undertaken, in addition to their education, in 1807, the name of the institution
was not changed until 1827, when it became
the Baltimore female orphan asylum, the
name being again changed in 1846, to the
Baltimore orphan asylum. The act of incorporation of 1807 provided that, " For the
orderly management of said school, there
shall be annually appointed nine discreet
female characters. . . ." The directors were
also given power to bind out children placed
in the school.

In 1813 the Boston asylum for indigent
boys was organized, for the purpose of "re- Boston
lieving, instructing, and employing indigent asylum for
boys." In 1835 the institution was consoli- indigent
dated with the Boston farm school society, boys, 1813.

which two years before had purchased Thompson's island, in Boston harbor, and opened an institution "for the education and reformation of boys who from loss of parents or other causes were exposed to extraordinary temptations."

In 1814 the orphan society of Philadelphia, apparently modeled somewhat after the New York and Baltimore societies, was organized "to protect, relieve, support, and instruct orphan children." In the following year, under the leadership of the wife of President Madison, the Washington city orphan asylum was established at the national capital. This institution has remained dependent upon private generosity, its only aid from public sources being a grant of land valued at $10,000 in 1832. The protestant orphan asylum of Natchez, Miss., was organized in 1816. The following year, three institutions were established, — the Poydras female orphan asylum, endowed by Julien Poydras, in New Orleans, St. Mary's female orphan asylum, of Baltimore, and the Roman catholic orphan asylum society in New York city, the latter two being the first catholic institutions in these cities.

The writer has not found it possible to prepare a complete list of the private institutions for children established in the United

Other institutions.

States.   Fewer than half of the states have
state boards of charities, and even the reports
of most of these boards give little information
concerning private institutions.   In several of
the largest cities, directories of charities are
published by the charity organization societies,
from which lists of children's charities in these
cities may be compiled.   The report on crime, List of
pauperism, and benevolence forming a part pioneer
of the eleventh census, 1890, gives in part ii, children's
pages 894–936, a list of benevolent institutions charities
in each state.   They are not classified, how- in the
ever; orphan asylums, hospitals, homes for States.
the aged, and other charities being grouped in
one table, and the name often giving no clue
to the nature of the institution.   Nor is there
any list of the institutions discontinued prior
to 1890, though the number would probably
be small, the longevity of organized charitable agencies being remarkable.   A writer has
pointed out, in *The Charities Review* for May,
1895, that of the nineteen charitable institutions in Boston sixty years before, only three
had ceased to exist, while of fifteen public
buildings and associations only five remained.

From all of the sources indicated above,
and by special correspondence, a table has
been prepared, which is believed to be rea-
sonably complete, showing the dates of the

organization of private charities for children during the first half of the century, as follows :

1727   Orphan asylum of Ursuline convent, New Orleans.

1738   Bethesda orphan house, Savannah.

1797   Society for the relief of widows and small children, New York.

1798   St. Joseph's female orphan asylum, R. C., Philadelphia.

1799   St. Paul's orphanage, P. E., Baltimore.

1800   Boston (female) orphan asylum.

1806   Orphan asylum society, New York.

1807   Orphan asylum, Baltimore.

1813   Boston asylum for indigent boys.

1814   Orphan society of Philadelphia.

1815   Washington city orphan asylum, Washington.

1816   Protestant orphan asylum, Natchez.

1817   St. Mary's female orphan asylum, Baltimore.

1817   Roman catholic orphan asylum, New York.

1817   Poydras female orphan asylum, New Orleans.

1822   Association for the care of colored orphans, Philadelphia.

1824   Asylum for destitute orphan boys, New Orleans.

1826   Roman catholic orphan asylum, Brooklyn.

1828   Female orphan asylum, Portland, Me.

1829   St. John's orphan asylum, R. C., Philadelphia.

1830   Orphan asylum, Utica.

1831   St. Vincent's orphan asylum, R. C., Boston.

1831   Orphan asylum, Albany.

1831   St. Vincent's female orphan asylum, R. C., Washington.

1831   Leake and Watts orphan asylum, New York.

1832   Farm school society, Boston.

1833   Orphan asylum, New Haven.

1833   Orphan asylum, Cincinnati.

1833   Orphan asylum society, Brooklyn.

1833   Children's friend society, Boston.

1833   Infant school and children's home association (now the Hunt asylum for destitute children), Boston.

1834   St. John's female orphan asylum, R. C., Utica.

1835   Children's friend society, Providence.

1835   Society for half-orphan and destitute children, New York.

1835   Orphan asylum, Troy.

1835   Nickerson home for children, Boston.

1836   Orphan asylum, Buffalo.

1836   Colored orphan asylum, New York.

1837   Foster home association, Philadelphia.

1837   St. Aloysius orphan asylum, R. C., Bond Hill, Ohio.

1838   Catholic male orphan asylum, Mobile.

1838   Shelter for colored children, Providence.

1838   Orphan asylum, Rochester.

1839   Protestant orphan asylum, Mobile.

1839   Children's home, Bangor, Me.

1840   St. Vincent de Paul male orphan asylum, Baltimore.

1840   Christ church asylum for female children, Baltimore.

1841   Southern home for destitute children, Philadelphia.

1843   New orphan asylum for colored youths, Avondale, Ohio.

1844   Male orphan asylum, Richmond, Va.

1845   St. Mary's home, R. C., Savannah.

1845   St. Peter's asylum, P. E., Baltimore.

1845   Onondaga county orphan asylum, Syracuse.

1845   St. Patrick's orphan asylum, R. C., Rochester.

1845   Protestant orphan asylum, Nashville.

1845   St. Vincent's orphan asylum, R. C., Albany.

1845   Manual labor school for indigent boys, Baltimore.

1846   Hudson orphan and relief association, Hudson, N. Y.

1846   Institution of mercy, R. C., New York.

1846   Society for the relief of destitute children of seamen, New York.

1847   Temporary home for the destitute (now the Gwynne temporary home for children), Boston.

1847   Orphan house, Poughkeepsie, N.Y.

1847   St. Mary's orphan asylum, R. C., Natchez.

1848   Protestant foster home, Newark.

1848   Orphan asylum, Newark.

1848   Jefferson county orphan asylum, Watertown, N. Y.

1848   St. Vincent's female orphan asylum, R. C., Buffalo.

1848   St. Patrick's orphan asylum, R. C., Baltimore.

1848   Protestant home for orphan girls, Baton Rouge.

1848   Children's friend society, Worcester.

1849   Children's mission to children of the destitute, Boston.

1849   German protestant orphan asylum, Cincinnati.

1849   St. Joseph's male orphan asylum, R. C., Buffalo.

1849   Orphan asylum, Chicago.

1849   Kentucky female orphan asylum, Midway, Ky.

1850   St. Vincent's asylum, R. C., San Rafael, Cal.

1850   Five Points house of industry, New York.

The various periods may be grouped as follows :

Founded prior to 1801		6
"	1801 " 1811	2
"	1811 " 1821	7
"	1821 " 1831	6
"	1831 " 1841	26
"	1841 " 1851	30
		77

New York early began to show a tendency to multiply institutions, under the influence of aid from the public treasury. With one seventh of the population of the country, the state included two sevenths of the institutions founded prior to 1851. It is not possible to trace the establishment of children's institutions after 1850 in detail. It may be stated that everywhere they increased in numbers and in diversity of character and objects. Not including some central and western states, from which returns have not been received, forty-seven new institutions were organized in the fifties, seventy-nine in the sixties (notwithstanding the civil war), and twenty-one in the first half of the seventies.

After 1850, institutions increased rapidly.

In the list of children's charities founded prior to 1850, there are several different types of institutions. One type was that founded by a group of people who were not neces-

Types of institutions.

sarily associated in any other organization, and whose activities in this direction seemed to be prompted solely by philanthropic impulses. Usually, however, it happened that these persons either were members of protestant churches or of none. Some form of religious observance, undenominational, but non-catholic, was usually provided for the children. In name, organization, and management the institution was not connected with any church organization. This type, well represented by the orphan asylum societies, would usually regard itself as non-sectarian, but by members of other than protestant churches it would be called sectarian and protestant. Another type was the orphan asylum organized as a distinctively religious institution, largely under the control of the church authorities, and usually under the immediate management of the religious orders.

Each form of organization has its peculiar merits and its disadvantages, but the reader who overlooks the difference between the two points of view above set forth will fail to understand some of the most powerful influences in the development of child-saving agencies in the United States.

A third type of institution appeared later,

The undenominational, as distinguished from

the distinctively religious institution.

the endowed orphan asylum, established usually by a bequest, and managed as a trust by a board of directors.   Such were the Poydras female orphan asylum in New Orleans, the Leake and Watts orphan asylum in New York, Girard college in Philadelphia, the McDonough school near Baltimore, and many others.   Among these, Girard college is worthy of special mention.

Endowed asylums.

Stephen Girard died in 1831, leaving property, then worth about $6,000,000, for the establishment of a college for orphans.   Evidently he had both charitable and educational objects in mind, for in his will he specified that, "As many poor white male orphans between the ages of six and ten years as the said income shall be adequate to maintain shall be introduced into the college as soon as possible."   The term male orphan has been construed to mean any fatherless boy whose mother has not remarried.   It was Mr. Girard's wish that boys who proved worthy should be kept until at least fourteen years of age, but not after reaching the age of eighteen. Unruly boys were to be dismissed.   Buildings costing nearly $3,000,000 were completed in 1847.   The endowment has greatly increased in value, the present value of the property of the institution being estimated

Girard college,

at $24,000,000, and yielding an annual net income of nearly $1,000,000. The institution opened with 100 boys on January 1, 1848, and the number steadily increased until on December 31, 1900, there were 1481 pupils. The boys are taught all branches that are suitable for children of their ages. It is, of course, not a college in the usual sense of the term, but is intended to fit boys for commercial and mechanical pursuits. The estate, which was left to the care of the mayor, aldermen, and citizens of Philadelphia, is administered by the board of city trusts, appointed by the supreme court of Pennsylvania and the city courts of Philadelphia. The grounds are surrounded by a high stone wall, and in many respects, notwithstanding the beauty of the buildings and environs, the college has a decidedly institutional appearance. The class of boys received includes many who otherwise would probably be admitted to orphan asylums and such institutions, with a proportion of those whose parents are in somewhat better circumstances.

Its beneficence is not to be doubted ; but when it is remembered that this institution has a larger endowment than any university in the land, it is to be questioned whether its founder did wisely in yoking together free education and free maintenance.   As an educational agency, even if it were to give the same sort of education as at present, it certainly could reach a very much larger number who need such instruction if it were simply a series of day schools.   On the other hand, solely as a charity it could be much more effective if freed from the restrictions imposed by the will, in the effort to make the proposed "college" an educational institution.   On the whole, it is to be feared that the name of its founder must be added to the already long list of those who have erred in trying to foresee the social needs of the future, and have tied up vast estates to uses which soon fail to meet the serious needs of the community.   Girard college is the largest and most important endowed children's institution in the United States, and probably in the world, but the example of Stephen Girard is not one to be followed by wise philanthropists.

an example of the disadvantage of combining free education with free maintenance.

Institutions for special classes of children also appeared.   The Philadelphia association for the care of colored orphans was organized by the society of friends in 1822, and was followed by similar institutions in Providence in 1835, in New York in 1836, in Avondale, near Cincinnati, in 1843, a second in Philadelphia

Institutions for special classes.

in 1855, and one in Brooklyn in 1866. Boston established no separate i.istitutions for colored children, but it is likely that then, as now, both colored and white children were received in many of her asylums. The institutions for colored children appeared in those localities in which the influence of the quakers, or friends, was strong.

About 1845 a day school, established by the society of friends for the children on the Cattaraugus Indian reservation near Buffalo, was reorganized as an asylum for orphan and destitute Indian children. For ten years it was supported by voluntary contributions, but from 1855 it received subsidies from the state. When state subsidies were abolished in 1875, it was reorganized as a state institution, and is to-day the only state institution in New York for the care of destitute children.

Another institution for a special class of inmates was the home for children of destitute seamen in the city and port of New York, established on Staten Island in 1846.

In founding children's institutions of a distinctly religious character, the catholics easily took the lead. Of the seventy-seven institutions established prior to 1851, twenty-one were under catholic auspices. In the fifties, a number of new institutions were

The religious institutions,

added to the list of those under the auspices of the protestant episcopal church — the orphans' home and asylum of the protestant episcopal church in New York city, in 1851, the church charity foundation of Long Island, in the same year, the charity foundation of the protestant episcopal church in the city of Buffalo, in 1858, the church home for orphan and destitute children in Boston, in 1855, the church home for children in Philadelphia, in 1856. The Lutherans established the Lutheran orphan home in Philadelphia in 1859, the evangelical Lutheran St. John's orphan home in Buffalo in 1864, the Wartburg farm school in New York city in 1866, and the Martin Luther orphan home in Boston in 1871. *among which the catholic predominated.*

The first Jewish institution for children was probably the Jewish orphans' home in New Orleans, established in 1856. This was followed by the Jewish foster home in Philadelphia in the same year, the New York Hebrew orphan asylum in 1860, the orphans' guardians society in Philadelphia in 1863, the Pacific Hebrew orphan asylum in San Francisco in 1870, the Hebrew orphan asylum in Baltimore in 1872, and others.

In 1851 a new type of institution appeared, in the New York juvenile asylum, organized through the efforts of the association for improving the condition of the poor, as the house of refuge had been organized a quarter of a century before by the society for the prevention of pauperism. The juvenile asylum aimed to receive, not simply destitute children, but also children who were neglected and in danger of moral ruin, and wayward children. It received children upon surrender by parents, and also upon commitment by the courts. It combined, in our opinion unfortunately, the functions of a home for destitute children, a training school for neglected children, and a juvenile reformatory. From the first it received substantial aid from public funds, both city and state.

Institutions for infants, combining the functions of maternity hospitals, infants' hospitals, and foundling asylums, appeared in the fifties. St. Mary's asylum in Buffalo for widows, foundlings, and infants was incorporated in 1852, but did not begin work until somewhat later. The nursery and child's hospital was established in New York city in 1854, and the New York infant asylum in 1865. The Massachusetts infant asylum was organized in 1867, the foundling asylum of the sisters of charity in New York in 1869, and the Philadelphia home for infants in

1871. Finding the mortality among babies cared for in institutions in cities very high, these institutions either established country branches, or placed the younger children at board in families. The sisters of charity in New York, the Massachusetts infant asylum, and the nursery and child's hospital adopted the latter plan, and the first and second still continue its use for large numbers of their children. The New York infant asylum and the nursery and child's hospital have each established country branches, one in Westchester county and one on Staten Island.

Temporary homes for children, as distinguished from orphan asylums in which the residence was more permanent, were established in Boston in 1847, and in Philadelphia in 1856. The sheltering arms, established in New York city in 1864, was designed especially for children of whom one or both parents are living, and are able to contribute toward the children's support.

In 1863 the New York catholic protectory was organized somewhat on the lines of the New York juvenile asylum. It received both boys and girls of all ages from two to sixteen years, and all classes of destitute, neglected, and delinquent children. It received substantial aid from the city and the state for the erection of buildings, and the cost of maintenance was, from the first, borne largely, and in later years wholly, by the city through a per capita grant made under a mandate of the state legislature. This institution grew with great rapidity, having 1944 inmates on October 1, 1875, and has since become the largest children's institution in the United States, if not in the world. A similar institution, but receiving boys only, was established near Buffalo in 1864.

Most of the above-mentioned agencies made more or less use of indenture, adoption, or placing out of children. Many of the orphan asylums adopted a rule that boys should be bound out at the age of twelve and girls at the age of fourteen. In the earlier history of Girard college many boys, upon leaving the institution, were bound out to farmers. As a rule, the orphan asylums seemed to regard the placing-out system rather as a convenient means of disposing of their older wards than as an essential part of the plan by which they were to benefit homeless children. There is little evidence of any adequate inquiry into the circumstances of the persons receiving children, or of any system of subsequent oversight. The children, after leaving the doors of the institution, were in

for both destitute and delinquent children.

Disposal of asylum inmates.

too large measure lost sight of. A few of the institutions, however, laid great stress upon the placing of orphan and permanently deserted children in families, and developed more or less satisfactory plans for finding homes for large numbers of children. Among such were the New York juvenile asylum (1851), the New England home for little wanderers (1865), and the New York foundling asylum (1869), all of which sent numbers of children to homes in the western states.

At the date of the establishment of many of the orphan asylums there was more reason for retaining children for considerable periods of time than in later years. The public-school systems had not yet been adopted, and it seemed necessary, in order to secure the proper education of orphan children, that they should be collected in institutions. With the establishment of public-school systems and compulsory attendance, not only in the cities, but throughout the rural districts, this necessity disappeared, though many institutions failed to recognize the changed conditions under which their work was carried on. This perhaps contributed to the fact that a new type of organization appeared.

Societies known as children's aid societies were organized in New York in 1853, Balti-

Placed-out children practically lost sight of.

Detention in institutions for educational purposes.

became less necessary with the advent of compulsory school attendance.

Organization of children's aid societies, for the direct placing in families of destitute children.

more in 1860, Boston in 1865, Brooklyn in 1866, Buffalo in 1872, and Philadelphia in 1882.

The New York society, organized through the efforts of the late Rev. Charles Loring Brace in 1853, addressed itself to the improvement of the condition of the poor children in New York in many ways: through the establishment of lodging-houses for news-boys and other homeless children; by day and evening schools for children who were not reached by the public-school system; by reading-rooms and religious meetings; and by sending homeless children to families in the country. The last of these plans is the only one which comes directly within the scope of this volume. This plan was, in brief, to send homeless children in groups of from twenty to forty to some point in the western states, where arrangements had been made for holding a large public meeting on the date of the arrival of the children. At this meeting the work of the society was explained, and people were urged to receive these friendless children into their hearts and homes. A local committee had been appointed to pass upon applications, and to see that none but respectable people, able to give good homes to children, received them.

In several important respects this plan differed from previous methods of placing out children by adoption or indenture. In selecting the territory offering the best opportunities for young people, even though at great distances from New York city, in appealing to the humanity of the country people rather than to their business instincts, in taking the young children rather than the older ones, and in boldly asserting that the ordinary experiences of life in an ordinary family are a better preparation for self-support and self-guidance than institutional training, — in these, and in other respects, the work challenges our admiration, for its boldness, its appreciation of the value of normal social forces, and its comprehensiveness. The children were received from the newsboys' lodging-houses, from orphan and infant asylums, from almshouses, and directly from parents. The results have undoubtedly justified the bold plans and large hopes of its founders. While it might be desired that fuller records had been kept and a more rigid supervision followed, there is satisfactory evidence that a very large proportion of the children sent out have become integral and useful parts of the growing western communities. A number have attained

The new method of placing out differed materially from the indenture plan.

Normal home life advocated as superior educationally to the institution.

Results of this work favorable.

considerable eminence in the professions; several have held important positions of public trust, one became governor of a territory, and one, governor of a state. We shall allude later to the work of the society after 1875. The statistics of children placed out have only recently been separated from those of families for whom transportation to a rural point was given, and for older boys for whose employment work was provided near New York city. The number placed in families averaged almost exactly one thousand per year for the twenty years 1854–1875. It is probably not too much to say that this work affected the child problem of New York city, for the twenty years prior to 1875, more strongly and beneficently than any other one factor.

An interesting though not extensive work is that of the orphans' guardians of Philadelphia (1863). The object of this society is to rear and educate Hebrew orphans by boarding them with a relative, or with some other worthy family, a member of the board of directors becoming the legal guardian of the child.

The children's aid society of Baltimore Baltimore. was founded in 1860 for the purpose of finding homes for destitute children. Ninety-eight children were placed in families during the first year. At first, only children from ten to fifteen years of age were received. Many of the children were received from the courts and magistrates, and on the ground that it was "an important adjunct to the police department," the city council appropriated to the society from $500 to $1000 annually; the remainder was received from private contributions. In 1871 Mr. Henry Watson bequeathed $100,000 to the society, which thereafter was known as the Henry Watson children's aid society. No further contributions of public or private funds were solicited for some years. The placing-out work was not largely increased, but a sewing school, a boarding home for working girls, and a lodging-house for adults and children were established.

The Boston children's aid society was organized in 1863. Its purpose, according to the act of incorporation of 1865, was that of " providing temporary homes for vagrant, destitute, and exposed children, and those under criminal prosecution, of tender age, in Boston and its vicinity, and of providing for them such other or further relief as may be advisable to rescue them from moral ruin." Apparently, the founders of the society were not quite clear as to just how they would

Evolution of the Boston society.

care for their children. Section 4 of the charter provided, with admirable caution, that "The directors shall have authority, at their discretion, to receive into their *asylum or care* such children of tender age as they may deem suitable objects of the charity intended by this institution." The directors were also given power to bind out children "in virtuous families," and to consent to their adoption. The first work of the society was the establishment of a temporary home in the country known as Pine farm. The first annual report of the society is largely a description of this farm school, although the sentiment is expressed several times that it is the purpose of the society to maintain "an oversight and influence" over the boys after they leave the farm. Fifty-two boys were received the first year, and twenty-three were discharged, of whom eight were placed in families in the country. In the third annual report of the society, we find the sentiment expressed by those in charge of the farm school that it is difficult to find places in families for the younger boys. The wish is expressed "that the society would authorize us to try the plan of paying moderate board in families in which we can trust them, and thus enable us to

Its farm schools, or temporary homes.

benefit a larger number." The reports of the society prior to 1875 tell interestingly of the work of an admirable temporary home or training-school in the country, but give comparatively little promise of the splendid development of preventive work and of boarding out and placing out carried on by the society in more recent years.

The children's aid societies organized in Brooklyn in 1866, and in Buffalo in 1872, devoted their energies rather to the maintenance of lodging-houses, newsboys' homes, and industrial schools, than to the placing out of children. The beneficent work of the children's aid society of Pennsylvania was not begun until 1882, and will be treated of in a subsequent chapter, as also will be that of the children's home societies.

CHAPTER IV

REMOVAL OF CHILDREN FROM ALMSHOUSES

Historical sources: "The removal of children from almshouses," by Homer Folks, *Lend-a-Hand*, September, 1894 (J. Stillman Smith & Co., Boston). Report of special commissioners to examine the penal, reformatory, and charitable institutions of the state of Michigan, and the methods of caring for such children in other states (Volume ii of joint documents of 1870, state printer, Lansing, Mich.). Reports of New York state board of charities, 1867–1876. Pauper children in poorhouses and almshouses in the state of New York: extracts from proceedings of boards of county supervisors, etc., 1861–1874 (20 pp., library of state charities aid association, New York). Report of the commission on the number and condition of dependent and neglected children in the state of Connecticut, January, 1883 (Tuttle, Morehouse, & Taylor, Hartford).

IN tracing the public care of children from 1801 to 1875, we noted the scathing arraignment of the care of children in almshouses by the select committee of the New York senate in 1856. From that time the conviction spread that the collection of children in almshouses had been a serious mistake. Ten years later, the first of a series of laws for the removal of children from almshouses was passed. In some cases a different system of

Laws excluding children from almshouses.

caring for children who were public charges was created; in other states, laws were passed prohibiting the sending of children to alms-houses, or their retention therein for longer than a certain period, usually thirty, sixty, or ninety days, leaving the local authorities to make such other provision for the children as they might elect. In briefest outline, these laws were as follows :

In 1866 Ohio passed a law authorizing the establishment of county children's homes, after a favorable vote by the people in each case, to be supported by taxation and man-aged by boards of trustees appointed by the county commissioners. Three such homes were established between 1866 and 1870, six during the decade 1870–1880, thirty-three between 1880 and 1890, and six since 1890. In 1883 a supplementary law was passed pro-hibiting the retention of children over three years of age in poorhouses, unless separated from the adult paupers. For many years the enforcement of the law was extremely inade-quate, as there was no penalty for its violation. In 1898 the age to which children may be kept in almshouses was reduced from three years to one year.

Ohio sub-stitutes county homes.

Massachusetts abolished the almshouse de-partment at the state primary school at Mon-

Massachu-setts

son in 1872, and thus separated destitute children from adults, so far as state charges were concerned. In 1879 a law was passed requiring overseers of the poor of cities to place destitute children over four years of age in families or asylums and provide for their maintenance. In 1887 it was provided that whenever the overseers of any city, except Boston, failed to comply with this law, the state board of lunacy and charity should provide for the children at the expense of such cities. In 1893 the laws of 1879 and 1887 were amended so as to relate to towns as well as cities.

Michigan was the first state to treat the matter in a really comprehensive, effective manner. In 1869 a commission, appointed by the governor, made an exhaustive inquiry into the condition of children in the county poorhouses, and the methods of caring for such children in other states. The report of the commission, submitted in 1870, stated that there were over 200 children under sixteen years of age in poorhouses in Michigan. The degrading influences of such surroundings were pointed out, and action for the removal of the children was suggested. The commission suggested the adoption of one of three plans: first, a state placing-out agency

establishes a state school for state charges, and requires the placing of local dependents in asylums or families.

The Michigan system,

by which dependent children should be removed from the county poorhouses and placed directly in private families; second, the removal of the children to private orphan asylums, to be supported therein at state expense until placed in families; third, the establishment of a state primary school "after the plan of that at Monson, Mass." The commission, while declaring itself strongly opposed to institutional life, favored the second plan as the best provision for the temporary care of the children. It also urged the importance of supervision of adopted or indentured children. The legislature proved to be more radical than the commission. It disregarded the many requests that were made for state aid to private institutions, and passed a law creating a state public school for dependent children, to which all destitute children in the state who were public charges were to be removed, and from which they were to be placed out in families as soon as possible. The institution was opened at Coldwater, in May, 1874.

In 1875 a law was enacted in New York, through the efforts of the state board of charities, supported by the state charities aid association and others, requiring the removal of all children over three years of age, not

combining a state public school with prompt placing out.

In New York,

defective in body or mind, from poorhouses, and directing that they be placed in families, orphan asylums, or other appropriate institutions, and that the public authorities make provision for their maintenance. This legislation was the culmination of a movement extending over some eight years. The state board of charities, created in 1867, found, on its first examination of the almshouses of the state in 1868, 2231 children in these institutions, 1222 being in county poorhouses and 1009 in the children's departments of the almshouses of New York city and Brooklyn. Efforts were made by this board and by other public-spirited citizens to induce the county boards of supervisors to make other provision for the children, either by placing them in families or by sending them to children's homes and paying their board. In some counties many of the children were, by one or both of these methods, removed from the poorhouses. Nevertheless, at the close of 1874 there were still 2066 children in almshouses. The number in county poorhouses had been reduced to 593, but in New York city and Brooklyn it had risen to 1473. The law of 1875 created no machinery for placing out or otherwise providing for the children. The local authorities very promptly complied

in the absence of proper placing-out machinery,

transfer was mainly to private asylums, where the children were supported at public expense.

with the law, generally by placing the children in orphan asylums, and within two or three years the plan of supporting destitute children at public expense in private institutions became the settled policy of the state. In 1878 the New York law was amended by reducing the age to which children may be retained in almshouses, from three years to two years, and by abolishing the exemption of defective children.

In 1878 Wisconsin passed a law requiring the removal of children from almshouses, but made no other provision for them until seven years later, when, in 1885, it established a state public school for dependent children, following closely the lines of the Michigan system.

Wisconsin follows Michigan.

In 1883 Pennsylvania enacted a law prohibiting the retention of children between the ages of two and sixteen years, unless feeble-minded or defective, in poorhouses for a longer period than sixty days. The county authorities, being left to make such provision for their children as they might choose, adopted various plans. Most of the larger counties entered into coöperation with the children's aid society of Pennsylvania, under whose care the children were boarded in families at the expense of the counties until permanent free homes were found for them.

Pennsylvania counties helped by the children's aid society.

Connecticut adopts county homes.

In 1883 Connecticut passed a law directing the establishment of a temporary home for children in each county, and prohibiting the retention of children over two years of age in almshouses. In 1895 a penalty for non-compliance with this law was provided. Unfortunately the law was amended in 1897, so as to permit the retention of children under four years of age in almshouses.

Rhode Island, a state school.

In 1885 Rhode Island established a state home and school for children, and in 1892 made mandatory the removal of all children from almshouses to the state home.

Maryland, subsidies.

In 1890 Maryland passed a law prohibiting the retention of children between the ages of three and sixteen years, unless mentally defective, in almshouses for a longer period than ninety days. The local authorities, as a rule, sent the children to private institutions, paying for their support.

New Hampshire, subsidies and placing out.

In 1895 New Hampshire prohibited the retention of children between the ages of three and fifteen, except the feeble-minded, in almshouses for a longer period than thirty days. The overseers of the poor and county commissioners were directed to place such children in orphan asylums or in families. A state board of charities was charged with the duty of enforcing this law.

In 1897 Indiana passed a law prohibiting the retention of children between the ages of three and seventeen years in any poor-house after January 1, 1898, for a period longer than ten days (made sixty days by the legislature of 1901). A state placing-out agency, under the direction of the state board of charities, was created by the same statute to assist and promote the placing out of children from the various county homes. Indiana, a placing-out agency.

In 1899 New Jersey created a state board of children's guardians, in which is vested the custody of all children who become public charges. The law also forbids the retention of children more than one year of age in almshouses for a longer period than thirty days. The children are to be boarded in private families until permanent homes can be found. New Jersey, boarding and placing out.

The delays in the removal of children from almshouses is a lamentable illustration of the slowness with which such reforms proceed. Thirty-five years have passed since Ohio enacted the first law in the United States looking toward the removal of all children from almshouses, but as yet barely a dozen states — about one fourth of the whole number — have followed her example, and even in these states the laws are not, in all cases, fully en- Only these twelve states so far have excluded children from alms-houses.

forced.   In 1897, and again in 1899, the Illinois legislature eliminated from pending bills
relating to the care of children, a provision
prohibiting their retention in almshouses.
Connecticut, as noted above, took a backward
step in 1897.   These are exceptions, however,
and the movement has steadily, though very
slowly, gained in momentum, and such legislation will, beyond doubt, become more general and more stringent and will be better
enforced as the years pass.

The census of 1880 showed that the actual
number of children in almshouses between
two and sixteen years of age, in the United
States, was 7770.   The earlier censuses did
not give this item of information.   The census
of 1890 showed that the number had been
reduced, during the preceding ten years, from
7770 to 4987.   Considering the increase of
twenty-five per cent in the general population, the decrease of thirty-six per cent in the
number of children in almshouses is not
without encouragement.   The number between two and sixteen years of age in almshouses to every 100,000 of the total population
was reduced from fifteen in 1880 to eight in
1890.   Included in the total of 4987 are
large numbers of defective children, and also
many children retained in so-called children's

asylums connected with almshouses, but in which the children are not immediately associated with adult paupers, a plan which is just a little less objectionable than keeping both classes in the same building. It is to be regretted that statistics on this point will probably not be given in the census of 1900.

Contrary to the general opinion, the states in which there were still large numbers of children in almshouses in 1890 are not confined to the south. In fact, as shown by the following table, the sixteen states which are the worst offenders in this regard include ten of the sixteen which comprised the union in 1801 :

mainly in the older states of the union.

NUMBER OF CHILDREN BETWEEN TWO AND SIXTEEN YEARS OF AGE IN ALMSHOUSES, TO EVERY 100,000 OF THE GENERAL POPULATION, 1890.

New Hampshire	46
Vermont	27
West Virginia	25
New Jersey	23
Virginia	19
Maine	18
Ohio	17
Rhode Island	16
Massachusetts	15
Indiana	15
Kentucky	14
Montana	12
North Carolina	10
Pennsylvania	8
Illinois	8
Tennessee	8

CHAPTER V

THE STATE SCHOOL AND PLACING-OUT SYSTEM

Historical sources and discussion : See article on state public schools for dependent and neglected children, G. A. Merrill, in report of committee on child-saving, national conference of charities and correction, 1893. Also reports of state public schools for dependent children : Michigan, 1874– ; Minnesota, 1885– ; Wisconsin, 1885– ; Rhode Island, 1885– ; Colorado, 1896– ; Montana, 1894– ; Nevada, 1869– ; Texas, 1889– ; also Iowa soldiers' orphans' home and home for indigent children, 1876– ; and Kansas state home for soldiers' orphans, 1887– .

Public systems other than almshouse care :

THE public systems adopted in various states for the care of destitute children outside of almshouses may be roughly classified as follows :

state schools with placing out,

(*a*) The state school and placing-out system, adopted by Michigan, Minnesota, Wisconsin, Rhode Island, Kansas, Colorado, Nebraska, Montana, Nevada, and Texas.

county homes,

(*b*) The county children's home system, adopted by Ohio, Connecticut, and Indiana.

support in private

(*c*) The plan of supporting public charges in private institutions, which prevails in New

York, California, Maryland, the District of Columbia, and to some extent in several other states.

(*d*) The boarding-out and placing-out system, which is carried on directly by the public authorities in Massachusetts; through a private organization — the children's aid society — in Pennsylvania; and has recently been undertaken by the state authorities in New Jersey.

Although Massachusetts established a state primary school at Monson in 1866, having collected there two years before all children from the other two state almshouses, and removed the larger part of the adult paupers therefrom in 1872, this institution was only for the care of the "unsettled" poor children. Each city and town still cared for its local poor, including destitute children, in its own way — often in the almshouse.

Michigan was the first state to establish an exclusive state system for the care of all destitute children who become public charges, by collecting them in one central institution, from which they are, as soon as possible, placed out in families. Neither the state nor the local authorities place any children in private institutions, nor make any appro-

[marginal notes: institutions, and boarding out and placing out. The Michigan plan.]

priations to private agencies. The "Michigan plan" has become known far and wide, and has been adopted by a number of other states. During the twenty-seven years of its existence, this system has followed closely the lines laid down by its founders. These have already been suggested in part. Children are committed by the judges of probate of the various counties, upon the application of the superintendents of the poor. Subsequent legislation authorized the commitment to the school of neglected and ill-treated children in the same manner. All such children become wards of the state, but may be returned to their parents by the voluntary action of the board of control of the school. The system is under the direction of an unsalaried board of control of three members, appointed by the governor and serving for a term of six years each, one member being appointed every other year. The state public school, located at Coldwater, is not unlike many other well-managed institutions on the cottage plan. At the outset, a system of county agents was established, the governor being authorized to appoint in each county an agent to investigate applications from families desiring to receive children, and to visit the children placed in homes in his

Children, both destitute and neglected, committed by courts, becoming wards of the state.

County placing-out agents provided,

county from any of the state institutions. These agents receive a per diem allowance, limited in certain counties to a maximum of $100, and in other counties, including large cities, to a maximum of $200 per year. There is also a state agent appointed by the board of control, whose duties are to investigate applications for children, and to visit children who have been placed out. Children of all ages under fourteen years are received at the school, and are retained only until, in the opinion of the superintendent, they are fitted to be placed in homes, and satisfactory homes are found. The average age of the 4807 children received from the opening of the school in May, 1874, to July 1, 1900, was six years and two months. Sixty-six per cent of the total number were boys. Among the number were 248 colored children and thirteen Indian children. About one-third of the whole number, or, to be exact, 1422, came directly from poorhouses, and 3385 from the homes of parents, relatives, or others. The census of the institution has varied from 150 to 250. In 1884 it reached 255. On June 1, 1900, it had fallen to 155. The expense of maintaining the school, including salaries of state and county agents, has ranged from $36,000 to

supplementing the work of a special state agent.

Statistics of the school,

$45,000 per year, being $39,340.90 for the year ending July 1, 1900. The number of children placed out in families, and remaining under supervision of the school, has varied during the past decade from 900 to 1200. The total number of children received since the opening of the school were accounted for on July 1, 1900, in the following manner :

showing 5000 children dealt with in twenty-six years,

Remaining in school July 1, 1900 .	. 155
In families under supervision .	. 1262
Adopted by families . . .	. 484
Girls who have married . . .	. 145
Died at the school or in homes .	. 167
Restored to parents . . .	. 575
Declared self-supporting . .	. 1109
Become of age	. 299
Returned to counties . . .	. 611
Total number received . .	. 4807

and a net decrease in the number of public charges during this time.

When the school was established there were about 225 children in the poorhouses of the state. Although the population of the state increased from 1874 to 1900 eighty-one per cent, and although laws have been enacted and enforced for the rescue of neglected and ill-treated children, who have thus become wards of the state and inmates of the state public school, the number of children who are public charges actually decreased from 225 in 1874 to about 200 in

1900, the latter figure including about fifty defective children in almshouses. The number of new admissions to the state public school last year was less than in any year since 1879.

Minnesota established a similar institution in 1885. One feature of the Michigan plan, the county agent system, was omitted. Reliance was placed upon state agents employed directly by and under the control of the school. In 1897 the county superintendents of schools were made ex-officio agents of the state public school. The census of the school has increased slowly but quite steadily. The average census for the year ending December 31, 1900, was 240, as against about 150 in the Michigan school for the same period. Three agents are now employed in finding homes for children and visiting them subsequently. The 2159 children received from the opening of the school to December 31, 1900, are thus accounted for:

Remaining in school, 1900	255
In families on indenture	1063
In families on trial	47
In families, adopted	77
Died in school or in families . . .	66
Returned to parents	105
Self-supporting	458
Returned to counties, being improper cases .	88
	2159

The average age of the children when received was slightly higher than in Michigan, being 8.16 years, as against 6.8 years in Michigan. Of the 1058 children in families on indenture, July 31, 1900, the following account is given:

more than half of whom are now self-supporting or doing well on indenture.

	No.	Per cent
In good homes, progressing steadily, doing well	695	66
Not so promising, or in less desirable homes, doing fairly well	275	26
Give no promise of becoming useful, doing poorly	88	8

This does not include 543 children now past eighteen years of age, of whom it is stated that 450, or eighty-three per cent, have grown into men and women of good character.

A special study was made in 1897 and 1898 of 106 children, who had passed seventeen years of age, and one or both of whose parents were known to have been of bad character. Personal visits were made in each case in order to gain full information. It was found that eighty-three per cent were young people of good character. The investigation covered all children of bad parentage placed in families and past seventeen years of age. It is interesting that the percentage of good results is precisely the same as among all chil-

Bad parentage apparently of little effect on placed-out children.

dren past eighteen years of age, without regard to character of parents.

Wisconsin established a state school in the same year as Minnesota, and also kept largely to the Michigan plan. The school was on the cottage plan, and was opened in November, 1886. The census has been as high as 300, but on September 30, 1900, was only 147. The legislature of 1901 provided for the admission of crippled and deformed children of sound mind, and of infants, the minimum age having previously been three years. It also required all children to be placed out within sixty days after admission, or the filing of a verified statement of the reasons for the failure so to do, a similar statement to be filed every sixty days thereafter until the child is placed out. The 2221 inmates received from the opening of the school to September 30, 1900, are accounted for as follows :

Wisconsin plan similar to that of Michigan.

Cripples and infants admitted.

Placing out within sixty days mandatory.

Over two thousand children dealt with in fifteen years.

Remaining in school, 1900 . . .	147
In families on indenture . . .	1038
Adopted	173
Escaped	62
Died	30
Returned to counties . . .	228
Of age	157
Transferred to other institutions . .	54
In families on expired indenture . .	332
	2221

Rhode Island established its state home and school for children in the same year, 1885, as Minnesota and Wisconsin. The institution was placed under the control of the state board of education, but in 1891 it was placed under the charge of a newly created board of control consisting of seven members. The statute establishing the school was very brief, and left substantially everything to the state board of education. An amending act, passed in 1888, declared that the object of the institution was to provide for neglected and dependent children not recognized as vicious or criminal. The board of education was authorized, in its discretion, to place children in families, and was made the legal guardian of all children admitted to the institution. Placing out is one of the objects of this institution, but because of the lack of placing-out agents, and also, perhaps, owing to the small size of the state and the greater difficulty of finding satisfactory free homes for some classes of children in the eastern states, the placing of children in families has not been carried on so largely as in Michigan, Wisconsin, and Minnesota. The 630 children received from the opening of the institution in April, 1885, to December 31, 1900, are accounted for in the following manner:

Rhode Island places out proportionately fewer children.

Six hundred dealt with in fifteen years.

Remaining in home, Dec. 31, 1900 .	.	150
Placed in families .	.	.	415
Returned to local authorities .	.	.	32
Died .	.	.	7
Ran away .	.	.	13
Sent to reform school	.	.	13
			630

Kansas established a state home for soldiers' orphans in 1887. As the applications for the admission of soldiers' orphans decreased, the institution was opened to other destitute children by a statute of 1889, which applied to the school the essential features of the Michigan system, except that the county superintendents of schools were made ex officio its county agents. Gradually the character of the institution has been assimilated to that of the state public schools above described. Of the 160 children in the institution in December, 1900, only fifty-one were soldiers' orphans. The state makes small appropriations to a number of private institutions, giving $3400 to six different institutions in 1901. Under a law passed in 1901, county commissioners are authorized to commit children to private societies for placing out children, and to pay such societies an amount not to exceed $50 for the expenses incurred for each child.

The soldiers' orphans' home of Kansas transformed to a school similar to that of Michigan.

Some subsidizing of private institutions.

Colorado.

Colorado established a state home for dependent children, which was opened in March, 1896. Prior to that time dependent children were county charges, and were either detained in almshouses or placed in private institutions at county expense. A state agent is employed for placing children in families.

Montana.

Montana has a state orphans' home, opened in September, 1894. Of the 230 children admitted from that date to December 1, 1900, 148 have been placed in families or returned to relatives. The annual report of 1898 expresses the opinion that it is better to develop an efficient placing-out system than to keep the children and teach them trades.

Nevada.

Nevada also has a state orphanage, established at an earlier date than any other state institution for destitute children except that of Massachusetts, since closed. It was established in 1869. Prior to this time the state had for some years made appropriations to a private orphan asylum. This appropriation was discontinued after the state orphanage was opened. The orphanage is under the control of a board consisting of the state surveyor, the state superintendent of public instruction, and the state treasurer. The census varies from seventy to one hundred.

Children are placed in families occasionally, but this is not regarded as an important feature of the work. Though a strictly state institution, it received a legacy of $5000 in 1886 for an industrial department.

Texas, too, has a state orphan asylum, opened in 1889. This institution is endowed by lands set apart for the purpose **Texas.** when Texas, having seceded from Mexico, was organized as an independent republic, about 1836. The census of the institution on September 1, 1900, was 304. The endowment very evidently tends to encourage the retention, rather than the placing out, of the children.

During, or just after the close of, the civil war, Iowa established three homes for soldiers' orphans. As the numbers decreased, **Iowa.** two of the homes were closed. In July, 1876, the name of the third was changed to "Iowa soldiers' orphans' home and home for indigent children," and it was opened to all destitute children who were public charges in the state. It was intended that all children in the almshouses should be removed to this institution, but the law was not obligatory and was not fully carried into effect. The census of the home was thus divided at various dates :

					Soldiers' orphans	Other destitute children
1879	.	.	.	.	98	44
1887	.	.	.	.	42	209
1897	.	.	.	.	297	190
1900	.	.	.	.	265	181

Nebraska.

The state of Nebraska made appropriations for a number of years to the home for the friendless at Lincoln, an institution under private management. The state gradually increased its control over the institution as it increased its appropriations, and in 1899 took entire charge of the institution. The governor appoints the superintendent, who conducts the institution under rules and regulations prescribed by the board of public lands and buildings. It is reported, however, that it remains practically a local institution, and is not likely to develop into a state institution for children such as exists in Michigan.

A total of eleven states following the Michigan plan.

Eleven states have thus established institutions for dependent children, following more or less closely the Michigan model. Among the undoubted advantages of this plan are the following:

1. It offers little or no inducement to parents to throw their children upon the public for support. The fact that the cus-

tody of the children is to be vested in state authorities, and that the children are to be removed to an institution at some distance, from which after a brief period they are to be placed in families, discourages parents from parting from their children unless such a course is really necessary. Nor does this requirement, as a rule, work unnecessary hardship. The board of control can relinquish to worthy parents the custody of their children, if such a course becomes desirable, and does so in numerous cases. Furthermore, the fact that sending a child to the state institution involves the transfer of its guardianship to the state authorities affords a logical and altogether satisfactory division of the field of charitable work, as between the state and private agencies. It is natural and proper that the private institutions should receive children for whom only temporary care is needed. Such a dividing line is not easily established in states in which the subsidy system has been adopted, or in which there is a county home for children under the care of public authorities in each county. The superintendent of the Minnesota state public school recently reports that "The most important development in private charities for children

Side notes: This system discourages parents from parting with their children.

Private charities enabled to limit their efforts to temporary relief.

in this state seems to be a complete change in the functions of such institutions. They have become places for the accommodation of children whose parents wish to place their children in an institution for a short time, until they can take them and care for them again themselves."

One institution less subject to expansion than a group of smaller institutions.

2. One institution, supported by the state, is much less likely to increase in size indefinitely than a number of similar institutions, each of which is apt to become a centre of local interest and of a local pride which is more enthusiastic than wise.

State administration more intelligent, and less partisan, than local.

3. The state is a more intelligent, resourceful, impartial, and efficient administrative unit than local political divisions. It commands a better grade of talent, and, as a rule, more ample resources. Its institutions are generally less subject to partisan influences than those of cities, counties, or towns.

The prompt placing out characteristic of the system

4. The placing-out system, which has been made the most important feature of the best state systems, restores the children more promptly than any other method to the normal life of the family and of the community. In the state institutions there are none of the incentives to retain children unduly, such as are apt to prevail in local institutions, or in private institutions receiv-

ing per capita allowances from public funds. The effective use of the placing-out system not only secures to the children the undoubtedly superior advantages of family life and training, but also diminishes correspondingly the public burden. The amounts spent by the states of Michigan and Minnesota for the care of destitute children seem almost ridiculously small when compared with the amounts expended in other states; yet there is every reason for believing that the needs of the destitute and neglected children are nowhere more adequately met than in those states.

both beneficial to the children and surprisingly economical.

The leading objections that have been urged against the state school system are: That it is subject to the influences of partisan politics, and all the evils of the spoils system; that the trustees, superintendents, officers, and teachers are likely to be selected, not because of fitness, but because of political services or influence; that with every change in the political control of the state, the trustees and officers are likely to be removed, and inexperienced persons of doubtful qualifications placed in charge; and that the plan does not enlist the coöperation and support of the better classes of citizens, who, it is presumed, do not participate actively in politics. These

Objections urged against the system.

are serious charges, if well founded. It is the opinion of the writer, after careful study of this phase of the subject, that some of the state schools for dependent children have not been wholly free at times from harmful partisan influences, but that such disturbances have been temporary, and have not seriously impaired the proper development of the system, nor seriously endangered the welfare of any considerable number of children. The Michigan school, after being practically free from partisanship for nearly twenty years, was suddenly, in 1891, deprived of its board of control and placed, with the other charitable and with the penal institutions of the state, under a newly created board of control of a different political complexion. On at least one other occasion it had passed through political upheavals in the state without disturbance. In this case, after two years, the former political conditions returned, and the separate board of control of the school was reëstablished. During the twenty-seven years of its existence the school has had nine different superintendents, though it is stated on the best of authority that only two of these changes have been due in any degree to politics, and on several occasions superintendents of a different political faith

Partisan influences have interfered at times, but only temporarily.

Political experiences of the Michigan school.

from the board of control have been appointed and retained in office. The new political control, created in 1891, discontinued the state visiting agent, — a most short-sighted step, which resulted in losing sight of a number of the placed-out children. It is a question, however, whether the disturbances to which the Michigan state school has been subjected by politics have been more serious than those from which many private institutions suffer, in a correspondingly long period, from the influence of managers of limited experience, or who give but little time or thought to their duties, or who are actuated by motives akin to those which too often prevail in politics. It is also clear that the board of control, three in number, is quite too small to insure continuity in policy under changing political conditions. A larger, more slowly changing board would be a safeguard.

The Minnesota institution has had a history of which any institution, public or private, might well be proud. Its original board of control has never been abolished or superseded by any other body. One of the original board of commissioners, appointed to select the site and organize the school, has been from the first the president of the board. A former state agent and assistant superintend-

Similar disturbances not unknown in private institutions.

The Minnesota school has been remarkably free from political interference.

ent of the Michigan institution was made the first superintendent of the Minnesota school, and has remained continuously in charge until the present, and has progressively and consistently developed its work. The esteem in which he and other workers in similar institutions are held by those interested in child-saving work in all parts of the country is indicated by the fact that he was appointed chairman of the child-saving section of the twenty-seventh national conference of charities and correction, while the president of the conference was a former superintendent of the Kansas state institution for children.

The Rhode Island institution is also believed to have been substantially free from partisanship; that of Wisconsin, somewhat less so. While the danger of political interference is a real and a serious one, it should be borne in mind that there is an increasing application of the merit system to public charitable institutions; that untoward influences of a character akin to partisanship are not lacking in some private institutions; that in some states public sentiment is such that it has become "bad politics" to interfere with state charitable institutions, and that the state system possesses advantages, enumerated above, which,

The state school system the distinctively American

in our opinion, outweigh the dangers arising from politics. On the whole, the state public school for dependent children is undoubtedly the distinctively American contribution to public systems of child-saving work.

contribution to public systems of child saving.

Several states, including Pennsylvania, Illinois, Kansas, Minnesota, Ohio, Indiana, Iowa, and Wisconsin, have established state homes for soldiers' orphans. Since these institutions were created to meet a special need which, let us hope, is not likely to recur, their work will not be considered in detail. The decreasing number of applications for admission to such institutions has already created an interesting problem as to their future. Kansas and Iowa have solved the problem by gradually converting their state soldiers' orphans' homes into state public schools for dependent children. Minnesota and Wisconsin abolished their institutions ; the latter state, after maintaining the institution from 1866 to 1876, turned the buildings over to her state university. Illinois could not do better than follow the example of Kansas and Iowa. Efforts in the same direction have already been made in Pennsylvania, though there is little need in that state of a state public school for dependent children, on account of the efficient

Soldiers' orphans' homes being abandoned or converted into state public schools.

work of the children's aid society. The increasing amount of the state subsidies to private orphan asylums and children's homes in Pennsylvania affords, however, a plausible argument for the establishment of a state institution of this character. Indiana, strange to say, maintained her soldiers' orphans' home and her school for the feeble-minded in the same buildings and under the same management until 1885, when they were separated.

CHAPTER VI

THE COUNTY CHILDREN'S HOME SYSTEM

Historical sources and discussion: For Ohio, see proceedings of the national conference of charities and correction, 1880, 1888, 1890; also reports of state board of charities, 1867–1871 and 1876– . Indiana: see reports of state board of charities, 1889– , and *Bulletin of Charities and Correction* issued by the board. Connecticut: see article on history of child-saving work in Connecticut, Mrs. V. T. Smith, in report of committee on child-saving, national conference of charities and correction, 1893; reports of state board of charities, 1873– ; also proceedings national conference, 1885, 1887.

SOME fifteen years before Michigan established her now famous state public school for dependent children, a kind-hearted woman, who had been touched by the forlorn condition of the twenty-six children associated with adult paupers in the Washington county (Ohio) almshouse, established, under her personal direction, a small home for children on a farm ten miles from the city of Marietta. The county commissioners placed the children from the poorhouse under her care, paying her a per capita rate of $1 per week for their maintenance. With a view to

Origin of the Ohio county home system.

securing similar care for children in the other almshouses of the state, a bill was presented to the legislature of 1864 authorizing counties to establish homes for children. These homes were to be wholly apart from almshouses and under the control of boards of trustees appointed by the county commissioners, and supported by public funds. The bill became law in 1866.

Subsequently, the state board of charities exerted a powerful influence in behalf of the establishment of such homes, with the result that from 1866 to 1899 fifty were established. The placing-out system, while provided for in the statute, was not made in fact an important feature of the original plan; very likely because the good woman through whose influence it was established had been drawn into the work through observing the cruelty to which an orphan child who had been placed in a family of low character was subjected. The county homes varied much in the extent to which they placed out children, but only one or two of them undertook such work extensively. In 1889 a law was passed authorizing each county home to employ a placing-out agent. In 1900 only two of the homes were employing agents, so far as could be ascertained, though about

Placing-out an unimportant feature of the plan originally.

half a dozen placed out children through the Ohio children's home society.

In May, 1901, forty-eight of the eighty-eight counties in the state maintained county homes, each under a separate board of trustees; five counties made separate provision for children, but their homes were under the immediate management of the board of infirmary (*i.e.* almshouse) directors; and nine counties maintained their destitute children in private institutions, the county commissioners paying a per capita price for their maintenance. In several of these nine counties property formerly owned by the county has been transferred to private societies which administer the homes under the laws of the state, very much as the county homes are administered. In twenty-five counties no homes, either public or semi-public, are maintained. These counties, however, make provision for their dependent children in the county homes of other counties. In one county children are boarded in families by the infirmary directors.

Homes established in more than half the counties of the state.

On April 25, 1901, fifty-one children's homes, including forty-five county homes, two semi-public, and four maintained by infirmary directors, reported a total of 2260 inmates, of an average age of a little over

Over two thousand children in these institutions.

nine years, and an average stay in the institution of slightly over three years. These homes reported 1186 children as placed in families from January 1, 1900, to April 25, 1901. The total number of children admitted to the county homes since their organization is estimated at 24,600, of whom it is thought that about thirty per cent have been placed in families. Exact statistics are not to be had. The average retention of children varied greatly in different institutions. No reports are given of the total number of placed-out children remaining under the oversight of the homes, and probably only fragmentary records are kept of the children after they are placed out; certainly there is no uniform system of supervision for such children. In Ohio, therefore, the county system has proved to be seriously lacking in securing uniform and effective action by the various local authorities.

In Connecticut a number of persons who had been active in the establishment of a private home for children caused a bill to be introduced in the legislature of 1882 prohibiting the retention of children in almshouses. The bill failed of passage, but a commission was appointed to inquire into the subject. Upon the recommendation of this commis-

About 25,000 dealt with in thirty-five years; perhaps one third placed out.

No exact records or close supervision of placed-out children.

Lack of uniformity.

sion, a law was passed in 1883 authorizing the establishment in each county of a temporary home for children, and such a home was opened in each of the eight counties of the state before January 1, 1884. The homes have, in each case, been removed from the sites first chosen, and their management has undergone at least one radical change. The present plan provides that each county home shall be managed by a board, consisting of three county commissioners, one member of the state board of health, and one member of the state board of charities. Admission is by the selectmen of a town, in which case the child is a town charge, or by a formal commitment by a judge of probate, or judge of a city or police court, in which case the child becomes a ward of the state, the guardianship being vested in the board of managers of the home and the expense of maintenance being borne by the state. While a majority of the boards of managers of the homes are county officials, the expense is borne very largely by the state, the remainder being paid by the towns. The state board of charities is authorized to recommend to the boards of managers suitable family homes in which children may be placed, and is authorized to visit children who have been placed out.

Homes in Connecticut planned to be temporary only.

Children committed either as town charges or as state wards.

Placing-out in charge of state board of charities.

Two agents are employed by the state board for this purpose. Under this plan of a divided responsibility, and of a number of local institutions, it is not strange that the numbers of children increased rapidly, from ninety-four in 1884 to 705 in 1900. One county home, to relieve overcrowding, has since 1896 boarded a number of its younger children in families, with satisfactory results. One county, after maintaining a home in two different locations, accepted the offer of a private asylum, and for the past ten years the children have been boarded in this asylum by the county board of management, at the rate of $1.50 per week. The 4629 children received from the opening of the homes to September 30, 1900, are thus accounted for:

Remaining in county homes, 1900 .	. 705
Placed in families	. 2555
Returned to friends (relatives) .	. 1724
Placed in other institutions . .	. 392
Died	. 99
Otherwise disposed of . . .	. 299
	5774
Duplicated in above reckoning .	. 1145
	4629

In addition to the county home system, the town of Norwalk maintains a home for children in a building formerly used as a town almshouse, and several towns board children in private asylums. A recent official report states in regard to the county temporary homes : " It is very difficult to preserve their temporary character, and the number of children in the homes increases steadily year by year." In 1898, at the instance of one of the city boards of charity, the legislature authorized the retention of children in almshouses until four years of age, instead of two years, as formerly. This was done to prevent overcrowding in one of the county temporary homes, but it was a serious backward step. A further backward step was taken in 1901 when the boards of managers of the county homes were authorized to board children in private institutions, the bill being proposed and urged by those who favor public support of children in institutions under the control of religious organizations.

Over-crowding causes retrograde legislation.

Subsidies to private institutions authorized.

Indiana, in 1881, authorized boards of county commissioners to establish orphans' homes, which were to be placed under the immediate charge of matrons. Boards of unpaid visitors were to be appointed, but no form of actual control was provided except by the county commissioners and the matrons. Subsequently, under legislative authority, the

Indiana had a heterogeneous system of county homes until 1897,

commissioners in some counties intrusted the management of the county children's asylums to "local associations." In 1901 there were forty-seven orphan homes receiving children who were public charges, from the ninety-two counties of the state. This includes four county boards of guardians and several private orphan asylums receiving public charges. No statistics concerning the operations of these asylums prior to 1896 are available. The constant increase in the number of children led to a movement in 1895 to establish a state school for dependent children; the actual result, however, was, in 1897, a system of state supervision of the county institutions, and the establishment of a state placing-out agency under the state board of charities. At the same time the law requiring the removal of children from almshouses was passed. The agent of the state board began by visiting the county homes and enlisting an interest in the placing-out system. He is authorized to visit children placed out from county homes, to remove children from county homes and place them in families, and to transfer placed-out children from one family to another or return them to asylums. At the end of three and one half years' work by the state agent

when the rapid increase in the number of inmates led to state supervision and a state placing-out agency.

618 children had been placed out by him, of
whom 472 remained in families under his
supervision.

The number of children in the county
orphan asylums receiving public aid on October 31, 1897, was 1401 ; the number of children in almshouses on the same date, 232, —
a total of 1633. The number remaining in
the asylums on October 31, 1900, was 1626;
the number in almshouses, forty-nine, a total
of 1675, and an increase of forty-two during
the three years. The fact that, notwithstanding the marked increase in the number of
children placed in families, there has been
no decrease in the number of children who
are public charges is striking. Since the
establishment of the state agency four county
homes have been established and four others
have been closed.

In some states in which no system is enforced by law, there are isolated instances of
county orphan asylums under public control.
There are two such in Pennsylvania, one in
Maryland, one in New York, and possibly
others.

The advantages that have been claimed
for the county system are, that it enlists the
interest of the best citizens of the various
counties; that it avoids sending the children

Six hundred children placed out so far,

but no diminution in census of the county asylums.

Isolated county homes elsewhere.

Advantages claimed

for the
county
system

to a distance (a doubtful benefit); and that the institutions can be kept smaller and therefore more homelike, and are less likely to institutionalize the children.

As a matter of fact, experience has clearly demonstrated that the system possesses none of these benefits, except, possibly, the first,

not justi-
fied by ex-
perience.

and that the local interest which is aroused is more enthusiastic than wise in regard to child-saving methods, and tends to the enlargement of the institutions as a matter of local pride. A number of children's institutions scattered over a state have an almost irresistible tendency to increase the numbers of children who become public charges; parents are much more likely to part from their children for unworthy or insufficient causes; the management lacks uniformity and efficiency; the officials of the various homes are less expert than those of state institutions.

The results are shown by comparison of the numbers of children cared for under the

Ratio of
depend-
ents to
general
population

state and county systems in adjoining states in which conditions are similar. Ohio has one child a public charge to every 1839 of the population; Indiana has one to every 1547; and Michigan only one to every 15619. Connecticut has one dependent child a public charge in every 1288 of the population; Rhode Island only one to 2857. (In each case the census of 1900 is used for general population.) The difference is not to be accounted for by the different percentages of urban population. Rhode Island has the largest percentage of urban population of any state in the union, eighty-one per cent, as against fifty-three per cent in Connecticut. Michigan has thirty-one per cent and Minnesota twenty-six of urban population as against thirty-eight in Ohio and only twenty-four in Indiana.

greatly higher than under state school system.

The argument that county institutions are smaller and more homelike than state institutions loses most of its force in view of the fact that the leading state institutions are on the cottage plan, and also because the state institutions are but little larger than a number of the county institutions. Three of the county temporary homes of Connecticut, three of those of Ohio, and one of Indiana are nearly as large as the state institution of Michigan, Wisconsin, or Rhode Island.

State institutions little larger than individual county institutions.

Another objection to the county system is that such of the children as are placed in families are placed as a rule at a very short distance from their former surroundings, thus making·interference by relatives easy.

The weakness of the county system is

further shown by the fact that both Connecticut and Indiana have already established state agencies for removing the children from county institutions and placing them in families, and Ohio is considering such a step. It is doubtful, however, whether a state placing-out agency can ever overcome the disadvantages of local control. The experience of Indiana and Connecticut simply demonstrates more clearly than before the need of centralization.

It is not too much to say that the county children's home system has been fairly and fully tried, and has been found wanting.

County system has to be reënforced by state placing-out agencies.

This system, on the whole, not successful.

CHAPTER VII

THE SYSTEM OF PUBLIC SUPPORT IN PRIVATE INSTITUTIONS

Historical sources and discussion : As to New York, see "Child-saving in New York," W. P. Letchworth, in report of committee on child-saving, national conference of charities and correction, 1893. "Homes for homeless children," extract from ninth annual report of the state board of charities, relating to orphan asylums and other institutions for the care of children (Weed, Parsons, & Co., Albany, 1876). "Dependent children supported by the city of New York, and proposed draft of bill to create a department for their care," *Lend-a-Hand*, March, 1886; report on the institutions for the care of destitute children in the city of New York, from nineteenth annual report of the state board of charities, 1886 ; report upon the care of dependent children in the city of New York and elsewhere, from twenty-third annual report of state board of charities, 1890, — all by Mrs. J. S. Lowell. Proceedings of conference on care of dependent and delinquent children in the state of New York, 1893 (publication No. 59, state charities aid association). Annual reports of the state charities aid association, New York, 1894– , also its publications Nos. 63, 72, and 73 ; "Public aid to private charities : a rejoinder," in *Charities*, October 7, 1899 ; also "What brought about the New York system for caring for dependent children ? Do these reasons still exist ?" by Homer Folks, proceedings first state conference of charities and correction, Albany, 1900. "Municipal subsidies to private charities," a report to the board of estimate and apportionment of New York city, by Comptroller B. S. Coler (Martin B. Brown Co., New York,

1899). California : see reports of state comptroller. District of Columbia : see reports of superintendent of charities, 1890–1900 ; reports of board of charities, 1900–1901; also report of joint select committee to investigate the charities and reformatory institutions of the District of Columbia (Government printing office, 3 volumes, 1897–1898). New Hampshire : see reports of state board of charities, 1895–   .

The subsidy system accidental rather than intentional.

IT is doubtful whether any state has adopted deliberately and intentionally the plan of public support in private institutions as a general state system. Usually it has been undertaken in various localities as a temporary expedient, and then gradually extended, until, by permission of the state, rather than by its direction, it has become the prevailing system.

Beginnings of the system in New York state.

In New York, public subsidies to private institutions began many years before the passage of the law for the removal of children from almshouses. In 1811 the state authorized the payment of $500 yearly to the New York orphan asylum, from the public funds derived from auction sales; the same favor was later extended to the Roman catholic orphan asylum, organized in 1817. The house of refuge for juvenile offenders, organized in 1824, was from the first largely supported by state funds. So far as known, no other state appropriations were made to orphan asylums until 1847, when, in addition to the sum of

$500 to each of the two asylums mentioned above, $3000 was appropriated by the state to be distributed among orphan asylums for the education of their inmates. The number of institutions receiving aid, and the total amounts granted, increased with considerable regularity for ten years, reaching a total of $50,000 in 1857. During the years immediately preceding and subsequent to the outbreak of the civil war, the amounts were reduced, being only $11,000 in 1861. In 1866 the sum of $55,033 was distributed among fifty-eight institutions; in 1870 $150,000 was appropriated to orphan asylums, to be divided among the counties in proportion to the total valuation of property, and within the county to be divided among the asylums in proportion to the number of their inmates. In addition to this, thirty-five institutions received specific appropriations, ranging from $500 to $5000 each. Many private charities besides orphan asylums received state aid. The propriety of prohibiting such appropriations was considered by the constitutional conventions of 1846 and 1867. The latter convention adopted an amendment looking in this direction, but the entire revision failed of adoption by popular vote. The total amount granted by the state

Growth in magnitude, until in 1872 nearly a million dollars were granted by the state.

to private charities increased rapidly from $95,000 in 1863 to $910,000 in 1872.

This rapid growth, and the "log-rolling" and other objectionable practices in the legislature growing out of the custom, were undoubtedly responsible for the fact that the constitutional commission of 1873 adopted an amendment prohibiting the state from using either its money or its credit in aid of any private undertaking, except in behalf of juvenile delinquents. This amendment was ratified by the people in November, 1874, and put a sudden end to the granting of state subsidies. Only one institution was seriously altered in character by this step. The private asylum for destitute Indian children was soon afterward reorganized as a state institution, and remains the only state institution in New York for destitute children.

About 1850 some of the cities, counties, and towns also had begun to make appropriations to such institutions, usually in the form of a per capita allowance for public charges, but in some instances in gross amounts. Various institutions in New York city, not wishing to depend upon the voluntary action of the city authorities each year, secured laws directing the city to pay them a certain sum per week for each child under

State subsidies suddenly cut off, in 1874, without serious injury to the institutions affected.

Local subsidizing commenced in 1850,

their care. These sums were at first much below the actual cost to the institutions, but various amending acts were secured increasing the rates of payment, and with the fall in prices after 1870, the city allowances came to be sufficient to meet the entire cost of maintenance, and in some cases to leave a considerable margin to be applied to the erection of new buildings or the reduction of indebtedness.

and subsequently made mandatory for New York city.

The passage of the children's law in 1875, directing that children be removed from almshouses and placed either in families or in institutions for children, gave new impetus to the system. No official authorities were created for placing children in families, and though it was hoped and expected by the framers of the law that it would result in a very great extension of the placing-out system, such has not been its effect. The word almshouse was held to mean any institution maintained by public officers for the support of the poor, whether connected with an almshouse for adults, or otherwise. Most of the 1473 children in the city institutions on Randall's island and the almshouse nursery in Brooklyn, who were not defective in mind or body, were sent to private institutions, though some were sent to families in the west through the children's

Removal of children from almshouses, 1875, resulted not, as had been expected, in increased placing-out, but in further growth of the subsidized private institutions.

aid society. Two of the smaller counties, and one small city, secured special laws authorizing them to establish children's homes apart from their almshouses, but so fully was the transition to a private system effected that of 34,729 destitute, neglected, and wayward children in institutions (not including hospitals) in the state on September 30, 1899, only 1186 were in public institutions, of whom 825 were in a state reformatory, 112 in a state asylum for Indian children, and 249 in local public institutions. Another important factor in the situation was the feature of the law which required children to be placed, when practicable, in institutions controlled by persons of the same religious faith as the parents of the children.

It is evident that this plan involved the maximum of inducements for the upbuilding of large institutions and for the discouragement of the placing-out system. The income of the institutions depended wholly upon the number of children received and the length of their retention. A large number of children could be supported at a less per capita rate than a small number. Being under the control of persons of their own religious faith, the institutions naturally commanded the confidence of the children's parents and of

Per capita payments encourage large institutions and long retention of inmates.

their spiritual advisers. The fact that the parents, by placing their children in institutions, were virtually receiving public aid was so disguised as not to be perceived, and many of the parents, particularly those of foreign birth, came to regard the institutions somewhat in the light of free boarding schools. The institutions, being in many cases under the control of religious bodies, naturally were inclined to retain the children until thoroughly instructed and trained in the faith, and also to receive as many as possible of the children who might otherwise be won over to other faiths. In fact, the largest of all the institutions was established because, in the words of one of its authorities, " Hundreds, yes, thousands of catholic children were lost to the faith through a system [of placing-out] which ignored such a thing as religious rights in the helpless objects of its charity." Sound morality and good public policy are on the side of keeping children who have received definite religious training and instruction under the influence of the faith in which they have been instructed. In regard to younger children, who as yet have no special religious training or convictions, it is also best, whenever practicable, to keep them under the influences of the faith of their

Public relief in this form disguised.

Sectarian interest a factor, through the religious provisions of the law.

fathers. The practical operations of the children's law, however, arrayed the denominational interest on the side of the upbuilding of institutions, as against placing children in families even of their own faith, and brought to its support the strong arm of the law and the ample resources of the public purse. New institutions were incorporated for the purpose of receiving these public funds, and there existed for a time what can be described only as a rivalry on the part of various institutions to secure the commitment of large numbers of children to their care. The result was inevitable; children's institutions of a size hitherto unknown were developed, and the number of dependent children increased out of all proportion to the population. From 1875 to 1900 the general population of the state increased fifty-five per cent; from 1875 to 1898 the number of children in institutions increased 139 per cent.

Rivalry for the control of children.

Census of institutions has increased more than twice as rapidly as general population.

Comparatively few of the children were placed in families, the great majority of them being returned to their parents or relatives, upon reaching a self-supporting age.

Little or no supervision was exercised over the few children placed in families, and none whatever over children returned to relatives, so that it is impossible to speak with any

No definite knowledge of the results of the institution training.

authority as to the essential character of the product of the institutional training. Extravagant statements have been made both for and against — the simple fact is that we do not certainly know.

Such in general was the New York system prior to 1894. Its distinctive features were most strongly emphasized in the larger cities. Certain exceptions should also be noted. Richmond county adopted the system of boarding children in families until free homes could be found, and in this way kept the numbers at a minimum. Erie county, alarmed by the growing expense for this purpose, has, since 1879, employed one, and later two, agents to place children in families. Certain of the older institutions, whose general lines of work had been well established before the law of 1875, have been comparatively unaffected by the new conditions, and not being wholly dependent upon the income from public funds, have been less subject to the tendencies of the per capita system. The institutions under religious control have naturally retained children longer than the undenominational institutions. Of 1935 children who, on September 30, 1894, had been supported by the city of New York more than five years in institutions, 1612 or 83 per cent were in

A few exceptions to the system of long retention under subsidies.

catholic institutions; 268 or 14 per cent in Jewish institutions, and 55 or 3 per cent in protestant or non-sectarian institutions. This was doubtless due partly to a lack of knowledge of the placing-out system, partly to the difficulty of securing catholic and Hebrew families, and partly to a desire to retain the children until firmly established in their respective faiths. A notable exception to the general rule is the New York foundling hospital (R.C.), which has placed a very large proportion of its children by adoption before they have reached the age of five years, and may justly be regarded as one of the largest placing-out agencies in the country.

The objectionable features of the New York system have been materially modified during the past seven years. The constitutional convention of 1894 made two important changes. It forbade the legislature from thereafter compelling cities, counties, or towns to make appropriations to private institutions, thus putting a stop to the mandatory legislation which left the city no choice but to pay fixed gross amounts or per capita rates to a large number of private charities. The courts held that this law was not retroactive in its effect upon earlier legislation, but in 1899 a law was passed authorizing the city to increase or

Mandatory legislation rendered ineffective.

diminish the amounts theretofore fixed by law to be paid to private charities. This virtually gives the cities and counties unlimited home rule in this matter.

More important than this, however, was another constitutional amendment, adopted in 1894, which provided that no payments should be made by any city, county, or town, for any inmate of a private institution, who is not received and retained pursuant to rules established by the state board of charities. This action by the constitutional convention was to say in effect that there were serious evils to be remedied, and to refer the whole subject to the state board of charities, giving that body quasi-legislative authority to deal with the subject. The rules established by the state board in 1895, and continued with few changes to the present, have as their most important feature a provision to the effect that only inmates shall be paid for from public funds who are accepted as proper public charges by the local authorities charged with the relief of the poor. Such officers already had power to place children in institutions as public charges. This rule gave them power, not to discharge children, but to discontinue the payment of public funds for any child. Other provisions of the rules require detailed

Payments made subject to rules to be established by the state board of charities.

reports concerning each inmate to the state board of charities, compliance with the public health law, etc. The effects of the adoption of these rules, and of the measures taken by the state board and the local authorities for their enforcement, have been altogether wholesome, and have held in check the tendencies above mentioned.

These rules act as a check on the subsidy system.

A review of the whole system shows that the number of children (destitute, neglected, and wayward, public and private charges) in institutions on September 30, 1875, nine months after the children's law took effect, was 14,773. This number steadily increased year by year until 1894, when it reached 33,558; it then decreased for two years, being 32,644 in 1896; during the next two years it increased to 35,404 in 1898; during the following two years it decreased, the number in 1900 being approximately 34,000. It is not possible to give separately the figures for delinquent children, since many of them are sent to the same institutions as the destitute and neglected, and separate statistics are not kept. Nor is it possible to give separate figures for those who are not public charges. This proportion is not large, however, and there is no reason to think that it varies much from year to year.

Statistics of the system.

The effect of the changes introduced in 1894 was most marked in New York city. Here the number of children in institutions receiving per capita allowances from the city increased steadily until 1894. From 1890 to 1894 there was an increase from 14,550 to 17,076. From 1894 to 1896 there was a decrease from 17,076 to 15,707. During 1898 the number increased to 16,927, but from 1898 to 1901 fell to 15,589. An analysis of the New York city figures shows that, as a rule, in institutions under the management of religious bodies the tendency to increase the census prior to 1894 was more marked than in others, and also that these institutions yield less readily to the restraining influence of the new constitution. The figures are as follows:

Effect in New York city of restrictive legislation, a reduction in census.

INCREASE IN CENSUS FROM 1890 TO 1894

	Number	Per cent
Catholic institutions	1858	18.6
Protestant institutions	198	6.5
Hebrew institutions	470	30.8
	2526	17.3

DECREASE FROM 1894 TO 1896

	Number	Per cent
Catholic institutions	539	4.5
Protestant institutions	507	15.6
Hebrew institutions	323	16.2
	1369	8.0

INCREASE FROM 1896 TO 1898

	Number	Per cent
Catholic institutions	912	8.0
Protestant institutions	252	9.2
Hebrew institutions	56	3.3
	1220	7.8

DECREASE FROM 1898 TO 1901

	Number	Per cent
Catholic institutions	1029	8.4
Protestant institutions	489	16.4
Hebrew institutions (Increase)	(180)	(10.4)
Net decrease	1338	7.9

Another factor which promises to have a marked influence upon the situation is the coöperation established in 1898 between the charity organization society of New York city and the department of charities (boroughs of Manhattan and the Bronx). The society is given an opportunity to examine all applications for the commitment of children by reason of destitution, and if it finds that the parents, or surviving parent, are of good character and so situated that it is desirable that they should be enabled to keep their children, it secures for them, in coöperation with the society of St. Vincent de Paul and the united Hebrew charities, the needed assistance in the form of clothing, groceries, fuel, etc., and places the family under the

Commitment of children obviated by temporary relief to parents.

care of one of its district committees. This
will undoubtedly reduce the numbers committed. The establishment in 1899 of the
catholic home bureau, to find homes in families for destitute children, is another important step in the improvement of the New
York system.

Placing-
out of
catholic
children.

The method of reception of children who
are to become public charges was, prior to
1884, generally by informal commitment by
overseers or superintendents of the poor, or
in cities by commissioners of charities. A
number of institutions, under special laws,
received per capita payments for children
received at their own volition directly from
parents. In 1881 the penal code authorized
the commitment of destitute, neglected, and
wayward children by magistrates. This custom in New York city entirely superseded
commitment by the charities department; in
Brooklyn both systems were in use; but in
other parts of the state the commitments
were generally by poor-law officers. In 1894
a special law for Kings county required
magistrates to refer applications for the commitment of children to the charities commissioner for investigation and report. A similar
provision, but limited to destitute children,
was included in the greater New York char-

Method
of commit-
ment of
public
charges.

ter, taking effect January 1, 1898, and is continued in the revised charter of 1901.

The custom of informal commitment by the charities commissioners was resumed in New York city in 1897, and is now the usual method of committing destitute children. In June, 1901, the reception of children over two years of age as public charges by surrender by parents was discontinued by a rule established by the state board of charities. The present tendency is toward the commitment of destitute children by the poor-law officers, and of neglected and wayward children by magistrates.

The state board of charities is the only board which is authorized by law to inspect the private institutions for children, and this body has done so regularly only in very recent years. It is not difficult, however, to secure permission to visit, through the courtesy of those in charge. There is no doubt that some of the private institutions are

admirably managed, and that most of them are at least fairly satisfactory as to the care and education of the children. Naturally there is great variation between different institutions, as each is under wholly independent control. Prior to 1886 contagious ophthalmia was very common, and many cases of blindness resulted, but in that year a law was passed prescribing minutely many matters relating to sanitation, examination and isolation of new cases, cubic air space in dormitories, distance between beds, etc. One notable instance of an institution organized to care for children under public allowances, which was managed for the personal benefit of one family, and in which the inmates suffered almost every form of neglect and cruelty, was discovered. Through the efforts of the state board of charities, and the health and charities departments of New York city, the institution was abolished in 1897.

It has seemed necessary to consider the New York system at length, because of its exceptional character and the large number of children supported in institutions in that state (from one quarter to one third of the entire juvenile institutional population of the United States), and because it is so complicated that it would be impossible in any less space to make clear the essential character and tendencies of the system.

California has a system somewhat similar to that of New York, except that the payments are exclusively from the state treasury, and there is no official control over the ad-

California,

mission or retention of the children. State appropriations to orphan asylums and homes for the aged have been customary ever since the admission of California into the union in 1850. Section 22 of article iv of the present constitution of California, adopted in 1879, prohibits the state from making appropriations to private charities, except "institutions for orphans, half-orphans, or abandoned children, or aged persons in indigent circumstances." The constitution also provides that whenever any city, county, or town shall provide for the support of orphans, half-orphans, or abandoned children, it shall be entitled to receive from the state the same pro rata appropriation as may be granted to institutions under church or other control. The statutes of 1880, still in force, provide that every institution in the state, conducted for the care of orphan, half-orphan, or abandoned children, shall receive from the state treasury the sum of $100 per year for each orphan child, and $75 per year for each half-orphan or abandoned child, provided that abandoned children must have been in the institution at least one year. The statute provides that children over fourteen years of age, or for whose specific support the sum of $10 per month or more was paid, should not be in-

exercising no official supervision, pays private institutions per capita allowances from state funds, on an unrestricted number of inmates.

cluded under the act; also that no institution with fewer than twenty inmates should be included. In 1883 the act was amended so as to include foundlings and other abandoned infants, for whom the state is to pay $12 per month, until they reach the age of eighteen months, after which the payments are to be at rates above mentioned. The provision requiring a census of twenty is declared to mean, in connection with infant asylums, twenty admissions per year. California has thus, in effect, told the private charities to take care of as many children as they like and for as long a time as they like, and that the state will pay the bills. Statistics in regard to the operation of the California system are not so complete as are those of the system in New York, but they show a steady increase in the number of children supported, or partly supported, by the state, and also that the appropriations to counties form a small portion, about ten per cent only, of the total appropriations for the support of children. About thirty-five institutions are now receiving state aid.

The result has been a steady increase in the number of children supported by the state.

The number of children supported, and the amounts paid by the state at various periods during the past fifteen years, are as follows:

	Children	Amount
First half of 1885	3393	$119,897.75
" " " 1890	4723	142,894.00
" " " 1895	5680	170,321.53
" " " 1900	7153	215,072.21

Of the total appropriations for the first half of 1900, the protestant and non-sectarian institutions received forty-four per cent, the Hebrew institutions three per cent, and the catholic fifty-three per cent. The numbers of each of the different classes of children in 1885 and in 1900 are as follows:

	1885	1900	Increase per cent
Orphans	775	959	23.7
Half-orphans	2217	5399	143.5
Abandoned children . . .	294	509	73.1
Foundlings	107	286	167.3
Total	3393	7153	110.8

The rate of increase,

The increase in the number of children supported by the state from 1890 to 1900 was more than twice that of the general population, 51.4 per cent; in the population of the state, 22.9 per cent. The steady increase in these appropriations has aroused considerable sentiment in favor of a change in the system. The state controller, in his report for the two years ending June 30, 1898, speaking of these appropriations, said: "I believe some steps must be taken to reduce this expenditure.

Either the law must be repealed, or the amount now appropriated must be reduced. I am not of a mind to recommend the former, but earnestly commend the latter to your consideration." The governor's message in January, 1899, however, stated that, " In view of the recommendations of the controller to change the laws relating to orphans and half-orphans, because of the large amounts expended therefor, I desire to call the attention of this legislature to the fact that in the past we have expended large sums for much less worthy purposes. In this connection I desire to state that we should extend the period for which orphans and half-orphans are cared for, from fourteen to sixteen years of age. There should not be any reduction in the sum allowed for the maintenance of these children." The divided sentiment of the state is thus clearly manifest. As a first step toward a reform of the system, a bill was passed by the legislature of 1899 for the creation of a state board of charities with general advisory and visitorial powers, but it was vetoed by the governor. A similar bill was defeated in 1901.

The subsidy or contract system has had a most interesting history in the District of Columbia. In 1832 congress gave a tract

has caused efforts to bring about a change,

but so far unsuccessfully.

District of Columbia.

of land valued at $10,000 to each of the two then existing orphan asylums, one being non-sectarian and one catholic. Neither of these institutions has to this date received any other aid from the government. In 1867 an appropriation of $5000 for maintenance was made to the home for soldiers and sailors' orphans. These appropriations were continued, and gradually the private contributions decreased. From 1874 congress also reduced its aid, and the institution after struggling for some years was disbanded, and the property turned over to the Garfield memorial hospital association. Since 1869 congress has appropriated yearly from $5000 to $24,500 to the home for destitute colored women and children. In 1872 $20,000 was appropriated to St. Rose's industrial school, and from 1887 to 1899 an annual appropriation was made to it for maintenance. In 1875 an abandoned almshouse was given over to the industrial home school, and since 1879 the institution has received a yearly appropriation for maintenance. Private contributions decreased, and from 1885 to 1896 the institution was practically dependent upon federal aid. In 1896 the private corporation was dissolved and a board of trustees, appointed by public authority, placed in charge. In 1877, 1879,

1881, 1887, and 1893, other institutions were added to the list receiving public aid.

The increasing amounts of such appropriations, and the difficulty experienced by the legislators in finding any satisfactory principle by which to determine what amounts should be given, led to an agitation for a change, which resulted in 1890 in the creation of the office of superintendent of charities. It was the duty of the superintendent to study the situation, make recommendations as to specific appropriations, and also as to changes in the general plan. The first superintendent, Prof. Amos G. Warner, appointed by President Harrison, became convinced within a year that the subsidy or contract system could not be reformed, but must be abolished. As a step in this direction, the board of children's guardians was created in 1892 as a public body, appointed by the judges of the district, to act for the district in its care of destitute children. The first agent of this board was called to that position from the post of state agent of the Minnesota state public school for dependent children. All grants to private institutions were reduced forty per cent, and this amount was given to the board for its work. All children becoming dependent upon the public were to be committed to the

The superintendent appointed to control the system recommends its abolition.

A board of children's guardians created to assume direct control of children.

guardianship of this board, which might place them at board in institutions or in families, or in free homes in families. Meanwhile, with the advent of the Cleveland administration in 1893, a superintendent of charities favorable Strong opposition develops, to the subsidy system was appointed. Strong opposition to the board of children's guardians arose; its appropriation was diminished by nearly one half; and several of the subsidies were restored in whole or in part. These conditions continued for three years, during which time, notwithstanding all the unfavorable circumstances, the work of the board increased in efficiency and proved its humane but the efficiency of the board's work and economical value. At the end of this period a joint select committee of both houses of congress made an extended investigation of the whole subject, and presented a voluminous report which was, on the whole, extremely favorable to the public board of children's guardians. With the advent of the McKinley administration, the agent of the board of children's guardians was appointed results in a steady increase in its powers and influence. as superintendent of charities, in which position his influence has naturally tended to strengthen the board of children's guardians and to restrict further the subsidy system. In 1897 the house of representatives passed a bill abolishing the subsidy system, but the senate forced a partial compromise. The same occurred in 1898, in each case the powers of the children's guardians being strengthened and its appropriations increased, while the number of private institutions receiving grants was reduced. By an act approved in June, 1900, the office of superintendent of charities was abolished, and in its place a board of five unpaid members, with a salaried secretary, was created. This had been recommended by the then superintendent of charities, and the new board has declared itself in opposition to the subsidy system. The board of children's guardians has been further strengthened, considerably more than half of the district expenditures for children being now expended directly through this board.

The subsidy system further discouraged by the new board of charities established in 1900.

The only other state in which the system of public support in private institutions can be said to be the prevailing one is Maryland. Here the state appropriates gross amounts, a total of about $20,000 per year, to eight or ten private institutions, and the city of Baltimore also makes appropriations of gross sums amounting to about $12,000 per year to some six institutions. Under the new charter which took effect in 1900, a city board of supervisors of charities was created

Subsidies in Maryland.

and given important powers as to admission, transfer, and discharge of children who are public charges in private institutions.

Oregon also makes appropriations in gross amounts to some six private institutions, a total amount of about $26,000 per year, and destitute children are placed in these institutions by county officials. In 1901 $12,000 was appropriated to be paid to institutions not receiving specific appropriations, for the support of orphans and foundlings, at the rate of $50 per annum each. Oregon thus seems inclined to follow in the footsteps of California.

In Pennsylvania the state appropriates gross amounts to a considerable number of children's homes, hospitals, and other institutions. These appropriations to children's institutions and societies have increased from $10,000 given to one institution in 1875–6 to $64,500 given to twenty-six institutions in 1899–1900. The institutions receiving these grants, however, do not as a rule receive destitute children from public officials, who in most parts of the state coöperate with one of the children's aid societies. The subsidy system is not the controlling factor in the public care of children in this state, but if it continues to develop, it is likely to give rise

Marginal notes:

Oregon's policy similar to that of California.

Subsidies not a predominant factor in Pennsylvania,

owing to the work of the children's aid societies, and the prohibition of

to serious disturbances in the present system.
Its growth has doubtless been greatly restricted by a constitutional provision prohibiting state appropriations to sectarian
institutions.

In Delaware the state makes appropriations of gross amounts to two institutions,
and one county, containing the city of Wilmington, also gives aid in gross amounts to
four institutions.

North Carolina grants aid in gross amounts
to two institutions, which, however, decline
to receive children from almshouses. One
county, Buncombe, has organized a children's
home as a public institution.

Maine makes appropriations of gross
amounts to several private institutions which
receive some children from almshouses. The
women's Christian temperance union of this
state is active in placing children from almshouses in families.

Milwaukee has an interesting history in
regard to subsidies. Although Wisconsin
has a state school to which Milwaukee
contributes its share of taxation, this city
continued until 1897 to board its destitute
children in a number of private institutions.
In 1897, on account of the increasing expense
and the undue retention of the children in

by establishing a county home,

the private institutions, this plan was discontinued, and the county established a children's home, under the direction of a board of trustees of four members, appointed by the chairman of the board of supervisors.

In response to an inquiry as to why the county established this institution, instead of sending the children to the state institution, a competent authority writes:

"The state school receives no children under three years of age, and only those of sound mind and body. The county had many ineligible under the second heading, and also a number for whom only temporary shelter was needed."

The city had been supporting 300 children in private asylums. When the county home was opened and notice was sent to the asylums to transfer the children thither, only a very few children, all of whom were defective, were sent, the asylums preferring to keep the children at their own expense. The county home, with a capacity of 125, has never been fully occupied. After it had been open about one year it had some seventy inmates. During the next six months, by placing out some children, and by returning others to their parents, the number was reduced to thirty. Since January 1, 1900, the

reduces the number of public charges seventy-five per cent.

census has varied from sixty to ninety, about one fourth of the number supported under the former plan. The system has been strongly attacked, and efforts have been made by institutions formerly receiving public funds to bring about the renewal of the custom, but thus far without success.

New Hampshire, not being proud of the distinction of having more children in almshouses in 1890 in proportion to its population than any other state in the union, passed a law in 1895 directing local authorities to place destitute children in orphan asylums, homes, or private families, and, as soon as practicable, to find permanent homes for them and make contracts for their education and support during minority, which contracts are subject to approval or rescission by the state board of charities, created by the same statute. Under this law, all the children, except a few who were defective, were removed to asylums or families. An effort to repeal the law was made by the local authorities in 1897, but the result was simply that the law was made more drastic and the powers of the state board of charities increased. The board was directed to visit the homes and families in which all such children were placed, and to assist the county and town

New Hampshire's system, under the direction of the state board of charities.

officials in securing homes for the children. As might be expected, there is a marked tendency to place the children in institutions rather than in families.

In January, 1900, a card record was made of every dependent child in the state. On December 1 of this year this record showed that 443 children under sixteen years of age were being supported at public expense. Of this number 238 were in private institutions, and were being paid for by counties at rates ranging from $1 to $1.50 per week; 113 were being boarded in families at similar rates; twenty-five were in state institutions; and sixty-seven (mostly feeble-minded or infants) were in almshouses. As there were but 184 children public charges in 1890 (all in almshouses), it would seem that New Hampshire, while justly entitled to great credit for removing the children from almshouses, might well study the experiences of New York and California. A successful system of volunteer visiting has been inaugurated, and in 1901 the state board of charities was given a paid secretary, who will devote his time largely to visiting the placed-out children and overseeing the work of the volunteer visitors.

In Tennessee, four or five counties make

Since the removal of children from almshouses the number of public charges has not been decreased.

Efforts to improve efficiency of placing-out work.

per capita appropriations to private institutions for the support of children.

Doubtless there are other instances of state,
county, or municipal appropriations to children's institutions not included in the above,
but if so, they are of small sums and do not
amount to a general system for the care of
children in any state.

The advantages claimed for this plan
are :

(*a*) That it removes the whole matter from
the influences of partisan politics and the
dangers of the spoils system. To most persons who favor the contract system, excepting
those who do so because of the importance
they attach to religious instruction, this consideration is doubtless the prevailing one.
The thought of entrusting the lives and the
training of young children to men who may
be drawn from the ranks of " ward heelers,"
is justly alarming to all thoughtful citizens.
As we have indicated, however, in our consideration of state systems, experience does
not show that state institutions for children
have suffered largely from partisan influences.
It has also to be borne in mind that private institutions which are largely dependent
upon the public for support are not always

wholly removed from partisan influences, and that public appropriations to private charities have more than once proved to be the source of serious political evils. The extent to which such appropriations are now used to strengthen a political organization in Pennsylvania were set forth in a remarkable manner in a series of editorials in the Philadelphia *Times* in July, 1901, one of which is reproduced in *Charities* of August 3, 1901.

The experience of Pennsylvania in this respect.

(*b*) That it enlists the interest of public-spirited and benevolent citizens, who, as managers of the institutions or otherwise connected therewith, will visit them frequently, give careful attention to their administration, and in many cases take an active interest in the welfare of individual children. There is some truth in this assertion, though many of these citizens might be equally interested if the institutions received no public aid. Nor are state institutions wholly lacking in power to attract the interest and elicit the active efforts of some of the best citizens in their communities.

Interest of private citizens in the children's welfare stimulated.

(*c*) That the removal of the children from all connection with poor-law administration and public officials saves them from being known in the community as "pauper children." This is clearly a great advantage as

Removal from the "pauper" stigma

compared with the almshouse system or any system in which the children are kept in institutions in any way connected with almshouse administration. This claim does not hold, however, in comparison with the state public-school system. It may fairly be questioned whether the attitude of the community toward the children in the state public schools is not distinctly more favorable than toward those in orphan asylums, protectories, and other similar institutions.

an important advantage, but attained under the state school system also.

(*d*) That it is economical. It is claimed that private institutions are more economically, not to say honestly, managed than public ones, and that the per capita allowance made by the public authorities is distinctly less than would be required to support the children in public institutions.

Cost per capita less in private institutions.

It is urged against the subsidy system :

(*a*) That it encourages parents to throw their children upon the public for support, because they naturally have much greater confidence in private institutions, especially when managed by persons of their own religious faith and vouched for by their spiritual advisers. This tendency is further strengthened by the fact that this plan creates a large number of institutions, scattered throughout

The subsidy system, however, encourages an undue number of parents to

the state, thus permitting children to be kept near their former homes and subject to frequent visitation by their parents. While this is an advantage in caring for children whose parents should be encouraged to visit them, it is a decided disadvantage in dealing with those who should be separated from their parents during their entire childhood.

(*b*) That it removes all incentive for keeping the number in the institutions small, either by careful sifting of applications for admission or by maintaining an active placing-out system. This is especially true under the per capita system when the per capita payment nearly or quite equals, or even exceeds, the cost of maintenance. This tends to result in an increase in the number of children in institutions, increasing indefinitely the public burden, and subjecting large numbers of children to the influences of institutional life, when they might better be cared for by their own parents or placed out in families for adoption. The history of the contract system in New York, California, and elsewhere, proves that it is difficult, though recent New York experience indicates that it is possible, to restrain these tendencies.

(*c*) The contract or subsidy system makes proper classification of children difficult. If

ask for relief from the support of their children.

Nor is there any incentive, under per capita payments, to keep the number in an institution small.

the institutions were all under one management, it would be easy to distribute the
inmates among them on some rational classification, which would aid in securing their
proper mental and moral training. This is
next to impossible when each institution is a
law unto itself.   One of the most serious and
persistent evils of the New York system is
the mingling of destitute, neglected, and delinquent children in the same institutions.

Proper classification difficult.

While the net results of the operations of
the various systems until very recently would
seem to favor the Michigan plan, it does not
by any means follow that it would be wise
for the states now having the contract system
to abolish it and adopt the state system.   On
the contrary, it is much better, especially in
New York, that the present promising efforts
to overcome the earlier defects of the contract system should be encouraged, and given
the fullest and fairest trial.   It is entirely
possible that these efforts may prove to be
permanently effective, and that a combination
of private effort and public aid may be worked
out, superior to any system now in operation.

Future modification may overcome these defects.

CHAPTER VIII

THE BOARDING-OUT AND PLACING-OUT SYSTEM

Historical sources and discussion : As to Massachusetts, see reports of state board of charities, 1875–   .
Reports of children's institutions department, Boston,
1896–   . Article by Mrs. A. B. Richardson in report of
committee on history of child-saving, 1893 ; also proceedings of the national conference, 1880, 1883, 1884, 1886, and
1889. "The proposed state children's bill : Why it should
be established," by G. S. Hale (Ellis, Boston, 1895). The
state primary school, closing report, 1895. Pennsylvania :
Homer Folks in report of committee on history of child-
saving, 1893. Reports of children's aid society of Pennsylvania, 1882–   . "The legal status of children indentured,"
Talcott Williams (Myers & Shinkle Co., Pittsburgh, 1896).
"The advanced American plan for homeless children,"
Talcott Williams, London *Times*, October 24, 1894. "Care
of dependent children in New York and Philadelphia contrasted," Anna T. Wilson, *State Charities Record*, December,
1891 (State charities aid association, New York). Proceedings of the association of directors of the poor, 1873–   .
New Jersey : report of the New Jersey commission on defective, delinquent, and dependent children, 1898 (Mac-
Crellish & Quigley, Trenton). Reports of state board of
children's guardians, 1899–   . Illinois : see annual report
of Illinois children's home and aid society, *Children's Home
Finder*, Chicago, August, 1901.

MASSACHUSETTS, Pennsylvania, and New
Jersey have systems of caring for destitute

children which differ from all the preceding, in that the children are, as a rule, boarded in private families until permanent free homes in families are found for them. These states differ radically in that Massachusetts and New Jersey do the work directly through public officials, while in Pennsylvania the counties, as a rule, work through a private society, the children's aid society of Pennsylvania.

It will be remembered that the opening of the last quarter of the century found Massachusetts with her state juvenile paupers collected in the state primary school at Monson, except that some seventy-five remained at the state almshouse at Tewksbury, and a less number at the third state almshouse, now called the state farm, at Bridgewater. There was also a state visiting agency charged with the supervision of about a thousand children placed out in families from the state primary school and the two state reformatories. The various cities and towns cared for their poor, adult and juvenile, as they chose. In 1879 the state work was reorganized, the state primary school and the state reform schools being placed under a board of trustees, and the visiting agency was abolished, its duties being assigned to the state board of health, lunacy, and charity, which board was also

Early history of the Massachusetts system.

State board of charity becomes responsible.

given general supervision over all the state charitable institutions, the hospitals for the insane, and the reform schools just mentioned. In addition to the work of the paid visitors, a system of visitation by volunteers residing in the localities in which the children were placed was organized. This was found to be of special value for girls over twelve years of age, and the volunteer visitation was gradually restricted to this class.

In 1882 the boarding out of children from the state primary school was authorized by law and was actually begun in December of that year. In the same year legislation was enacted for the commitment to the custody of the state board of neglected children (between three and sixteen years of age) by the courts; the board was also authorized to board children in families directly, *i.e.* without passing through the primary school. In the following year legislation was enacted for the commitment to the board by overseers of the poor of infants under three years of age. All these children were, as a rule, placed temporarily in the state primary school, and later placed out in families, with or without board. From time to time laws have been enacted extending the classification of children committed to the custody of the state board of

Boarding out authorized, 1882.

charity.   In 1880 a law was enacted for
the commitment of foundlings to its care.
These children were, after 1884, placed
directly in families at board.   Gradually, as
the boarding-out and placing-out systems
developed, it was found possible to decrease
the numbers remaining in the state primary
school.   In 1876 this institution sheltered
485 children; on September 30, 1894, the
number had been reduced to 121.   The number of children boarded in families had meanwhile increased to 582, and the number
self-supporting in families to 1459.   By 1894
the state board of charity had placed so many
children from the state primary schools in
families that the abolition of the school was
possible, and in 1895, at the suggestion of the
trustees of state institutions, the buildings
were given over to the state to be used as a
hospital for epileptics, most of the remaining
children being placed in families at board.
Since that date Massachusetts has cared for
its destitute and neglected children who are
state charges wholly in families, and boarding places have been secured for a few of the
younger children committed to the reform
schools.

Notwithstanding the new classes of children who have been added to the state list,

By exten-
sion of
boarding-
out and
placing-
out work

the state
school
becomes
unneces-
sary, and is
abolished,
1895.

the number maintained at state expense has increased only from 1142 in 1876 to 2051 in 1900, including, in both years, inmates of reform schools, while the number of children under the supervision of the state, but self-supporting in families, increased from 1000 in 1876 to 1691 in 1900. The percentage of juvenile state charges in institutions, in free homes, and in boarding homes, in 1876 and in 1900, are as follows : [1]

	1876 Per cent	1900 Per cent
In institutions	51	15
In families without board	47	45
In families with board	2	40

In the city of Boston, destitute and neglected children were maintained in 1875 at the house of industry (almshouse and workhouse) on Deer island, except that the older pauper boys were in one wing of the house of reformation. Although probably not in actual association with adult paupers, the fact that they were on the same island and under the same authorities, associated the two classes in the public mind. In 1877 a distinct advance was made by the removal of the boys

[1] This whole matter is very clearly set forth in a chart opposite page 40 of the twenty-second annual report of the state board of charity.

to what had been the Roxbury almshouse, but which now became the Marcella street children's home. On March 1, 1878, there were 618 children under the care of the city — 160 "pauper children," 128 neglected children, 120 truants, and 210 juvenile offenders. In 1881 another advance was made by removing to a building near the Marcella street home, and thereafter reckoned as a part of it, the pauper and neglected girls from Deer island. This marked the final separation, territorially, of destitute children from pauper adults in Boston, although they remained under the same administrative control until June, 1897, when the children were placed under the control of a board of seven unpaid trustees. About 1889, the city also began to board out the younger children, especially infants. Agents were employed also for finding free homes for children. On January 31, 1898, there were 420 children under supervision by the city children's department in free homes, and 325 in boarding homes. On the same date there were only 160 children in the Marcella street home, the number having been reduced from 321 earlier in the year, by the extension of the placing-out and boarding-out systems. Later in the year, in November, 1898, the Marcella street home was discontinued alto-

Boarding out commenced in 1889.

Abandon-
ment of
the chil-
dren's
home,
1898.

Further
advance in
classifica-
tion.

gether, the children being placed out in families. Thus by a natural development of the institutional and placing-out systems, side by side, the city of Boston, in 1898, followed the example of the state, which, four years earlier, had abandoned its state primary school, both city and state thus arriving by gradual stages at the plan of caring for all destitute and neglected children in family homes. The parental (truant) school, which had been differentiated from the house of reformation on Deer island in 1877, was removed to West Roxbury in May, 1895, another step in classification. On December 31, 1900, there were under the care of the department 1396 children, as follows:

Dependent and neglected children
> boarding in families 430
> in free homes in families 305
> in various institutions
>> (mentally defective) 133
>> 868

Truants in parental school 196
Juvenile offenders
> in house of reformation 88
> in free homes in families 43
> with relatives on probation . . . 154
> elsewhere 47
>> 332
>> 1396

In the cities and towns of Massachusetts, other than Boston, destitute children are under the charge of overseers of the poor, and are either kept in almshouses, or placed in families to board or in free homes, or boarded in institutions. Children cannot be legally retained in an almshouse for a longer period than two months unless they are (1) under four years of age; (2) under eight years of age, with their mothers; or (3) so defective in body or mind as to render their retention in the almshouse desirable. In a few instances the children are cared for through the Boston children's aid society. The state board of charity is charged with the duty of visiting, at least once each year, children supported by cities and towns. If children are retained in almshouses contrary to law, the state board is authorized to remove them therefrom, and to charge the cost of their support to the town of their settlement. The number of children fully supported by city and town authorities March 31, 1900, was as follows:

Various provisions in other communities of the state.

Restrictions on almshouse care.

In town almshouses	192
In other institutions (mostly municipal children's homes)	189
In private families	733
	1114

The number of children supported by the state on September 30, 1900, not including inmates of reform schools, was 1493.

Massachusetts thus supports nearly one and a half times as many children as its cities and towns, including Boston. For some years the state board of charity has recommended that the system be unified and that all destitute and neglected children become wards of the state, supported from state funds, and under the control of the state board of charity. A long step in this direction was taken in 1900 by the enactment of a law authorizing this board to provide for dependent children, without regard to "settlement," at the request of parents, guardians, or overseers of the poor; also requiring courts and magistrates to commit destitute and neglected children to the state board, unless the local overseers of the poor object. The logical outcome would seem to be an exclusive state system in the near future.

There was in 1895 a considerable movement for making the state board of lunacy and charity a strictly supervisory body and for creating a state children's department, which should be known as the children's bureau, with trustees appointed by the governor, their work to be under the supervision of the state board of

The majority of children now state wards;

and the tendency is toward exclusive state care.

Supervisory and executive functions

charity. This failed to pass the legislature, and the executive care of the children in the state board's custody or care remains without supervision by any independent board. On July 1, 1898, the state board reorganized its work by abolishing its previous departments of indoor and outdoor poor, and creating a superintendent of state adult poor and a superintendent of state minor wards, thus collecting all children in its custody under one administrative control.

not differentiated under the state board.

Pennsylvania, when the "children's law" was passed in 1883, left the local authorities to provide for the children as best they could. Although the state subsidizes many private institutions, it does so on the general ground that they are doing good and presumably preventing persons from becoming public charges, and not because the institutions receive and care for public dependents. The county system of poor relief prevails in some forty-nine counties, the town system in eighteen of the most sparsely settled counties. By a happy coincidence, there had been organized, a year before the passage of the children's law, the progressive children's aid society of Pennsylvania, which at once offered to assist the local authorities in caring for their children. In many of the counties, including the large

Pennsylvania, after excluding children from almshouses, 1883, leaves the counties to shift for themselves.

cities, this offer was accepted, and the resulting plan may, with exceptions noted later, be regarded as the Pennsylvania system. The children's aid society has at no time in its history conducted an institution, but has relied wholly upon the boarding-out and placing-out systems, except for feeble-minded or persistently vicious children, or for those needing hospital treatment. The coöperation with the city and county of Philadelphia has been its most important work. The destitute children who are accepted as public charges by an agent of the charities department are either sent directly to the office of the society, or sent for not more than sixty days to the children's asylum across the road from the almshouse. They are placed at board in families, selected by the society, and nearly always in the country. The city pays the society $2 per week for their care while boarding. The society pays the families from $1.75 to $2.50 per week, besides providing for clothing, medical attendance, and other expenses. While boarding, the children are visited by an agent of the city department and by the society's agents, both of which endeavor to find free homes for such of the children as are not to be returned to their parents. Catholic children

The children's aid society helps, by boarding out and placing out.

This coöperation effective in Philadelphia,

are, however, generally sent to catholic institutions, the city agent retaining control of them and returning them to parents or relatives, or placing them in free homes, as circumstances warrant. Under this plan the number of children supported by the city has remained very small, in fact is very little in excess of the number of children in the almshouse seventy-five years ago. On May 22, 1826, there were 145 children in the children's asylum at the almshouse; on December 31, 1900, the city was supporting seventy-five children in private families, ninety-five in private institutions, and twenty-eight in the children's nursery, practically a department of the almshouse, though not in the same buildings. The cost to the city is proportionately slight, and the children in free or boarding homes are undoubtedly under the most favorable circumstances for their development. That the system thus outlined has been most humane and beneficent in its effect upon the children under its care is undoubted. That it has reduced the public expenditure to a minimum is also true. The element of weakness in the plan, regarded as a system for the state, is that it is dependent upon voluntary coöperation between the local officials in sixty-three counties and a private society, — or

and the cost to the city very slight.

rather several societies, since the original society has divided into several branches, the parent society remaining by far the largest and most active. Five separate branches secured state appropriations in 1899. This renders it impossible to secure a uniformly efficient system in all parts of the state. Two counties built children's homes under the control of their poor authorities, two others board out their children under their own care, while eleven counties place their children in institutions with per capita payment for their care until free homes are found. Even Philadelphia places its catholic children in institutions, and since 1895 has placed a considerable proportion of its protestant children in a private children's home instead of in families under the care of the children's aid society. Admirable as the coöperation between the children's aid society and certain of the counties has been, it does not cover the state as a whole, and, it is to be feared, lacks the elements of authority and permanency.[1]

The system lacks, however, the elements of authority and permanency.

In New Jersey until 1899 destitute children were city and town charges, and were provided for either by being kept in the almshouses, as they were to the number of about

---

[1] The work of the children's aid society for other than public charges will be alluded to later.

500, or being placed in families by indenture, or by being placed in private institutions at a per capita rate, the latter plan, however, not being used extensively. In 1895 the governor appointed a commission to investigate the subject. This commission reported to the legislature of 1897 a bill for the creation of a state board of children's guardians. The bill failed of passage in 1897, but became a law in March, 1899. Under this act the governor appoints a board of seven persons, to whose custody all children becoming public charges are to be committed. The children are to be placed in families at board until free homes can be found. Their board is, however, to be paid by the counties from which they come.

A board of children's guardians established in New Jersey in 1899.

When the law was enacted there were 403 children in the almshouses in the state, 255 of whom were in the Hudson county (Jersey City) almshouse. The freeholders of this county opposed the operations of most features of the act for two years. By November 1, 1900, the board of guardians had secured the removal of all children, except a very few defectives, from all the other almshouses of the state, having been instrumental in securing the return of 309 children (104 from Hudson county) to parents or relatives, and

Most of the children in almshouses returned to relatives;

in placing 111 children in families, with payment for board in some cases. In May, 1901, the freeholders of Hudson county discontinued their opposition, and the board of guardians removed the 160 children then in the almshouse, with the exception of eighteen defectives. There are now no children except defectives or very recent admissions in the almshouses of New Jersey; there are under the supervision of the board of children's guardians ninety-six children in free homes in families and 164 children boarded in families and thirty-four boarded temporarily in institutions. The number of children becoming public charges has been greatly reduced during the past three years.

The states of Illinois and Missouri, notwithstanding their large cities, have been singularly backward in making any public provision for destitute and neglected children. Neither state forbids the retention of children in almshouses. In Illinois the poor, including children, are a county charge, and children are kept in almshouses, placed directly in families, placed in the care of placing-out societies with a per capita allowance — usually $50 — for expenses of placing out, or, especially in Cook county (Chicago), placed in private institutions, where they are paid for

the balance placed or boarded out.

Illinois has no specific system for the care of dependent children.

by a per capita rate. The number of children so supported is not large, owing, perhaps, to constitutional limitation of such appropriations. An unsuccessful effort was made in 1888 to secure the establishment of a state public school for dependent children. In 1899 a law framed by the Illinois children's home and aid society was enacted, covering the general subject of the commitment and care of destitute, neglected, and delinquent children. The law defines these classes of children, specifies the courts which shall deal with them, requiring a separate court in Chicago, regulates the procedure, and provides for commitment to a suitable state institution, a reputable citizen, an industrial school, or an association for the care or placing out of children, or for placing the child on probation. "Associations" for the placing out of children are given legal recognition and authority to act as guardians of children; the approval of the state board of charities is required for their incorporation, and they are to be subject to visitation by that board, and are to make annual reports thereto. While the law has many admirable features, it stops short of providing any public system for the care of the destitute and neglected children whose status it defines and for whose com-

The children's law of 1899

defines and provides for the commitment of destitute and neglected children,

but provides no public system for their care.

mitment it provides.   It might easily lead to an extension of the contract system as it exists in New York.   It creates a decentralized system of coöperation with private institutions and societies, the results of which will depend largely upon the merit and efficiency of such societies.

Conditions are much the same in Missouri as in Illinois, except that many destitute children are sent to the reform school maintained by the city of St. Louis.

Illinois law copied.

Laws similar to the Illinois law were enacted in the state of Washington in 1900 and in Kansas and Pennsylvania in 1901.

Other states, having no public systems.

In the states not already mentioned in this and preceding chapters there are no public systems of caring for destitute children except outdoor relief, almshouses, and occasional placing out in families either directly or through a placing-out society.   This list includes the following states: Alabama, Arkansas, Florida, Georgia, Idaho, Iowa, Kentucky, Louisiana, Mississippi, North Carolina, South Carolina, South Dakota, Tennessee, Utah, Vermont, Virginia, West Virginia, and Wyoming.

CHAPTER IX

LAWS AND SOCIETIES FOR THE RESCUE OF NEGLECTED CHILDREN

Historical sources and discussion: "What should be the relation between a society for the prevention of cruelty and child-caring agencies," read before the international humane congress, 1893, reprinted in *Altruistic Interchange*, January, 1897. Reports of societies for the prevention of cruelty to children: New York, 1875– ; Philadelphia, 1877– ; Boston, 1878– ; Illinois humane society, 1877– . For court decisions in litigation between the New York society for the prevention of cruelty to children and the state board of charities see the *Quarterly Record*, June, 1900 (State board of charities, Albany). See also reports of board of children's guardians, Marion county, Indiana, 1889– . "The board of children's guardians," C. B. Martindale, in proceedings of first Indiana state conference of charities and correction, 1891. "Baby-farming," F. A. Burt, report to the conference of child-helping societies, Boston, November 28, 1892, published in *Lend-a-Hand*, January, 1893.

THE statutes in force prior to the opening of the nineteenth century indicate that children rarely became the subjects of public care except because of the poverty of their parents, or their own wrongdoing. The statutes of Massachusetts did, indeed, in a special poor law, passed in 1735 for the city of Boston,

Beginnings of care for neglected children.

because that town had "grown considerably populous and the idle and poor much increased among them," provide that when persons "were unable, or neglected to provide necessaries for the sustenance and support of their children," such children might be bound out by the overseers, and that "where persons bring up their children in such gross ignorance that they do not know, or are not able to distinguish, the alphabet, or twenty-four letters, at the age of six years," the overseers might bind out such children to good families "for a decent and christian education." We have no knowledge as to how many children were actually bound out under this remarkable statute. Numerous instances are found in the statutes of various states from 1790 to 1825, authorizing the binding out, or commitment to almshouses, of children found begging on the streets, or whose parents were beggars. A general statute to this effect was passed in New York in 1824. From about 1825 there came a more and more general recognition and practical application of the principle that it is the right and duty of the public authorities to intervene in cases of parental cruelty, or gross neglect seriously endangering the health, morals, or elementary education of children, and to remove the chil-

The duty of the public to intervene in cases of cruelty or neglect recognized after 1825.

dren by force if necessary, and place them under surroundings more favorable for their development. Such action, prompted by philanthropic instincts, finds justification in the fact that neglected childhood is a danger to the state. Step by step statutory authority has been gained for the rescue of neglected children; the definition of the term has been made more and more precise, and at the same time more inclusive; agencies have been created for the enforcement of these laws; and institutions established for the care of the children. The law amending the charter of New York city, passed in 1833, provided that the mayor, recorder, or any two aldermen, or two special justices, might commit to the almshouse, or other suitable place, for labor and instruction, any child found in a state of want or suffering, or abandonment, or improperly exposed or neglected by its parents or other person having the same in charge, or soliciting charity from door to door, or whose mother was a notoriously immoral woman. It has been commonly supposed that these statutes were of much later origin. New York in 1833,

The Massachusetts law of 1866 provided that children under sixteen years of age who, by reason of the neglect, crime, drunkenness, or other vices of parents, were suffered to be Massachusetts in 1866, growing up without salutary parental control and education, or in circumstances exposing them to lead idle and dissolute lives, might be committed by the proper court to the place designated for such purpose by the city. In 1882 a law was passed providing for the commitment of neglected children, between three and sixteen years of age, directly to the custody of the state board of charity.

In 1877 New York, at the suggestion of the society for the prevention of cruelty to children, passed a law entitled an act for the protection of children and to prevent and punish certain wrongs of children, which was in part adapted from the industrial school act of England. Subsequently, these provisions were embodied in the penal code, and have from time to time been extended.

Statutes of somewhat similar character have been enacted in nearly all the states of the union. One of the best is that of Michigan, passed in 1889. The sections describing the classes of children who may be committed, because of ill-treatment, to the state public school are drawn with great detail, and are among the most comprehensive that have found place in the statute books. In Michigan such cases are tried before the judges of probate.

The care of neglected as well as destitute
children has been a motive in the founding of
many of the private and public child-saving
agencies from the early part of the century.
The juvenile reformatories, though established primarily for actual offenders and to
prevent the commitment of such to prisons
with adults, received also neglected and destitute children, and their charters in many cases
authorized the commitment of such children
to them.   The fifth annual report of the New
York house of refuge, 1830, says: "The
legislature has very much enlarged the objects of our institution. . . . If a child be
found destitute; if abandoned by its parents,
or suffered to lead a vicious or vagrant life;
or if convicted of any crime, it may be sent
to the house of refuge." We have already
noted that early in the seventies neglected
children were being committed to the pauper
institutions of Boston.   Separate statistics.of
the pauper and neglected children have been
kept by Boston from that time to the present.
The state schools for dependent children,
though originally established for destitute
children, have at later dates been authorized
to receive neglected children.   In New York
the penal code enacted in 1880 authorized the
commitment of various classes of neglected

Neglected
children
committed
to reforma-
tories and
to pauper
institu-
tions.

children to "any incorporated charitable or reformatory institution."

The enforcement of laws for the rescue of neglected children, as well as the enactment of further legislation, received a great impetus from the organization of societies for the prevention of cruelty to children, the first of which was established in New York city in 1875. Curiously enough, societies for the prevention of cruelty to animals were in existence for eight years before similar societies for the protection of children were organized. The American society for the prevention of cruelty to animals was organized in New York city in 1866, similar societies followed in Massachusetts and Pennsylvania in 1868, in Maryland and Illinois in 1869, and in many other cities in 1871. The New York society for the prevention of cruelty to children was organized in January, 1875, and incorporated in April, 1875, under a general law passed that year for the incorporation of such societies. Other societies followed in the order named:

Societies for the prevention of cruelty to children, originating in New York in 1875.

1875, Rochester.	1878, Baltimore.
1876, Portsmouth.	1879, Buffalo.
1876, San Francisco.	1879, Wilmington, Del.
1877, Philadelphia.	1880, Brooklyn.
1878, Boston.	1880, Richmond county, N.Y.

In some cities, societies, originally incorporated for the protection of animals, added to their objects the protection of children. In others, new societies, often called humane societies, were organized for both purposes. The total number of societies in the United States in 1900, devoted exclusively to the protection of children, or to the protection of both children and animals, is 161.[1] In 1877 the societies for the protection of animals organized the American humane association, which holds an annual convention for the discussion of topics relating to the prevention of cruelty. Societies for the protection of children were admitted to this association in 1887.

Humane societies, protecting both children and animals.

The primary work of these societies has been that of investigating cases of alleged cruelty or neglect, and the presentation of the facts to the courts authorized to consider such cases. In New York, but not elsewhere, so far as known, unless in exceptional cases, the society for the prevention of cruelty to children has, in its coöperation with the courts, included also the investigation of cases of destitution.

The New York society has had an excep-

[1] See list in report of New York society for the prevention of cruelty to children, 1900.

tional history. Its first annual report stated that there were already in existence many institutions and societies for the care of children, but that it was not their business to seek out and to rescue children whose lives were rendered miserable by constant abuse and cruelty. The laws for the prevention of cruelty to children were considered ample, but it was nobody's business to enforce the laws. To this task the new society addressed itself. In addition to seeking to discover cases of cruelty and neglect, it stationed agents in all the magistrates' courts, to investigate all cases involving children, whether for destitution, neglect, cruelty, or waywardness. Through these agents it has advised the magistrates, not only as to whether commitment should be made, but as to what institutions the children should be committed to. Subsequently, the children were placed under the care of the society pending investigation, and the agents of the society were given the powers of police officers. Though the power to discharge the children was vested in the managers of the institutions, they, often regarding the society as the real authority through which the children had been sent to them, usually did not discharge the children either to their parents or by

The New York society investigated all court cases involving children, and advised the magistrates as to the commitment of the children.

adoption or indenture, without consulting the society, and in some cases took no action in reference to discharge until so requested by the society. This society thus became, by 1890, the factor which actually controlled the reception, care, and disposition of destitute, neglected, and wayward children in New York city, thus practically controlling the lives of an average number of about fifteen thousand children, and an average annual expenditure for their support of more than one and one half million dollars. Its influence has done more to strengthen and perpetuate the subsidy or contract system, as it existed prior to 1894, than any other one factor. Since additional powers have been conferred upon the charities commissioners by the state board of charities, acting under the revised constitution, the activities of the society, so far as destitute children are concerned, have been somewhat restricted.

Ultimately it came to control the entire disposition of all classes of children coming before the courts.

Its influence, which tended to perpetuate the subsidy system, restricted since 1894.

These societies have, in a number of large cities, provided temporary shelters for children coming under their care. As a rule the societies have been at first supported wholly by private funds, but latterly the societies in New York, Philadelphia, Wilmington, Brooklyn, and probably other cities, have received some aid from public sources.

Temporary shelters provided.

The influence of the "cruelty" societies as a whole has been in favor of the care of children in institutions, rather than by placing them in families.   So far as known, none of the societies have undertaken the con-
Placing
out not
employed
by these
societies
exten-
sively.
tinued care of the children rescued by them, but all have turned them over to the care of institutions or societies incorporated for the care of children.   By a vigorous enforcement of the laws authorizing the commitment of vagrant, begging, and various other classes of exposed children, they have very largely increased the numbers of children becoming wards of public or private charity.   Usually they have not coöperated to any extent with placing-out societies, perhaps because of being continually engaged in breaking up families of bad character, but have rather become the feeders of institutions, both reformatory and charitable.   The New York society during 1900 placed six children in homes or situations ; during the same period 2407 children were, upon its recommenda-tion, committed to institutions.   Constantly occupied with questions involving the cus-tody of children, they have, not unnaturally, preferred to place the children rescued by them within the walls of institutions, where possession is at least nine points of the law,

rather than to trust to a measure of uncertainty necessarily involved in the placing-out system. Without detracting from the great credit due to such societies for the rescue of children from cruel parents or immoral surroundings, it must be said that their influence in the upbuilding of very large institutions, and their very general failure to urge the benefits of adoption for young children, have been unfortunate. Probably their greatest beneficence has been, not to the children who have come under their care, but to the vastly larger number whose parents have restrained angry tempers and vicious impulses through fear of "the Cruelty."

Their influence best as a moral restraint on parents who would be cruel if they dared.

As indicated by their name, the societies for the prevention of cruelty to children are private corporations; their boards of managers are independent of official appointment. In only one state have governmental bodies been created to perform the duties elsewhere assumed by these societies. In the state of Indiana, a law of 1889 authorized the appointment of boards of children's guardians in townships (changed in 1891 to counties) having a population more than seventy-five thousand. In 1893 the law was made applicable to counties having more than fifty thousand population, of which there are

Local boards of children's guardians in Indiana, to protect against neglect and cruelty.

four in the state, in all of which such boards have been organized. Each board is composed of six persons, three of whom must be women ; the members are appointed by the circuit court. The boards not only investigate cases of alleged cruelty and neglect, and bring such to trial, but also undertake the subsequent oversight of the children, placing them in temporary homes, managed directly by the boards, or in institutions managed by others, or in families. A bill introduced in 1899 to make possible the appointment of such boards in counties having less than fifty thousand population failed of passage, but in 1901 a new but similar law, applicable to all counties, was passed.

The Colorado humane society was made by the legislature of 1901 "a state bureau of child and animal protection " and was given an appropriation of $3000 per annum for two years. It remains under private control, but three state officers are made ex officio members of its board of directors.

Colorado
humane
society.

CHAPTER X

PRIVATE CHARITIES FOR DESTITUTE AND NEGLECTED CHILDREN, 1875–1900

Historical sources and discussion: Reports of New York children's aid society, 1875– . "Country homes for dependent children," C. L. Brace (New York, 1898). Reports of Boston children's aid society, 1875– , and of boys and girls' aid society, Portland, Ore., 1885– . Reports of McDonough farm school (near Baltimore); Samuel Ready asylum, Baltimore ; Cincinnati children's home; Cleveland orphan asylum; and Rose orphan home, Terre Haute. Concerning the George junior republic, see *Outlook*, May 31, 1896 ; *American Journal of Sociology*, November, 1897, and January, 1898 ; *Journal of Education*, January 4, 11, and 18, 1900 ; *Puritan*, February, 1901 ; annual reports ; and the *Junior Republic Citizen*, published monthly. For discussion of comparative advantages of institutions and placing-out methods see : "Thoughts in an orphan asylum," Rabbi S. Schindler, *Arena*, November, 1893 ; "Advantages of institutions in the education of destitute children," Mary M. Cox, Philadelphia, 1887 ; "The responsibility of states to their dependent children," Mrs. M. E. Cobb (J. H. Franklin & Co., Fall River, 1888) ; "The shady side of the placing-out system," L. P. Alden, proceedings national conference, 1885 ; "Some developments of the boarding-out system," *The Charities Review*, March, 1893 ; "Care of dependent children," address, published in report of the Baltimore charity organization society, 1894 ; "Why should dependent children be reared in families rather than in institutions ? " in proceedings convention of superintendents of the poor of New York, 1895. Information in regard to individual institutions may be found in the directories of charities published in New York, Chicago, Boston, Philadelphia, Baltimore, Buffalo, and San Francisco. See also "Annual reports of child-caring organizations," *Lend-a-Hand*, October, 1893, and "State supervision of child-caring agencies," proceedings national conference, 1895. Agency for providing situations for destitute mothers with infants, annual reports, 1894– (State charities aid association, New York).

Private charities adapt themselves to varying public policies in the care of children.

THE development of private charities during the last quarter of the century has been variously affected in different states by the policies adopted by the public authorities for the care of children who are public charges. Where public institutions, especially state institutions, have been established for the care of children permanently separated from their parents, the private charities have gradually turned their attention to the temporary care of children, or to the care of some special class of children not fully provided for by the public, or to the development of special lines of instruction, emphasizing their educational rather than their charitable features. Where the subsidy plan has been adopted, the institutions wholly supported by private funds have usually ceased to be an important factor in the situation, and the subsidized institutions have increased in numbers and size, without much specialization in purpose. The plan tends to increase the number of institutions receiving about the same classes of children and caring for them by the same methods. A tendency to differentiation and specialization of private charities is undoubtedly better for the children and for the community.

During the early part of the last quarter of the century, children's institutions multiplied rapidly in all parts of the country. Forty were incorporated in New York alone in the fifteen years, 1875–1890. Since 1883 the consent of the state board of charities has been necessary for the incorporation of such institutions, and several needless and unworthy applications have been denied. In Philadelphia, only nine new institutions were incorporated in the interval 1875 to 1893, the last date for which the figures are available. Four of the nine were under the charge of various protestant denominations. In Boston, some eleven institutions, none of them large, and all of them entirely supported by private funds, have been organized since 1875. Several of these have recently employed placing-out agents, or have established coöperation with the Boston children's aid society. The Massachusetts infant asylum, which at first received state aid, has for many years been supported wholly by private funds.

They have increased rapidly since 1875, until the last decade.

Although exact statistics are not available, it seems certain that there has been a marked diminution in the number of new institutions organized during the last decade.

This seems to be due largely to the influence of the agencies which have favored the placing-out system, and to the remarkable success which has attended that system in many states. The New York children's aid society has continued its placing-out work to the present, though its coöperation with public authorities very greatly decreased after about 1875, the principal reason being that, inasmuch as the society declined to take into account the religious faith of the children in selecting homes, it met with violent opposition from many sources. The children placed out by it in recent years have been received largely through its lodging houses, or from protestant institutions, or from parents.

One of the most influential of the placing-out societies has been the Boston children's aid society. The principal work of this society from 1863 to 1885 was the maintenance of an excellent farm school for wayward boys, known as Pine farm, with an oversight of the boys placed in families or returned to their parents from this school. The

The later decrease due to the growth of placing-out agencies.

The Boston children's aid society

report for 1884 notes the need of an additional farm school, and also of sending some
children directly to country homes. In 1886
a country home in which a few boys had been
boarded was developed into a second farm
school, and a third was established soon after.
The girls under the care of the society were
sent directly to families. The number of
destitute and neglected children not requiring even the training of the farm school, but
who could be placed directly in private families, rapidly increased. Some of these children were placed in free homes, many
received wages, and others were boarded in
families. This society was among the first to
develop a careful, systematic, and satisfactory plan for the investigation of the character and circumstances of families applying
for children, and for the supervision of children placed in families, and has exerted a
powerful influence in raising the standards
of placing-out work, not only in Massachusetts, but also in other states. On October
1, 1891, 255 children were under the care of
this society in families, sixty in the three
farm schools, 168 in their own homes, and
twenty-seven in institutions. In 1892 one of
the three farm schools was discontinued, one
third of its pupils being sent to the other

passes from maintaining farm schools to direct placing out.

The society's system of investigation and visitation noteworthy.

farm schools, and the remainder, with one exception, placed in families. In 1896 a second, and in 1899 the third and last farm school was closed, because the improved provision by the state and city, coincidently with the development of the society's other methods, made them unnecessary. The number of children under the care of the placing-out agency December 31, 1900, was 281, of whom 146 were in boarding homes, eighty-seven in free homes, thirty-four were receiving wages, and fourteen were otherwise placed. The important work done by this society in promoting needed legislation, and through its bureau of information, its probation agency, home libraries, and other agencies for improving the condition of children in their own homes does not fall within the scope of this volume.

The coöperation of the children's aid society of Pennsylvania with public authorities has already been described. In addition to this, it receives a large number of needy or semi-wayward children directly from parents, and some from magistrates, all of whom are supported by voluntary contributions, from which source the funds for the running expenses of the society are also met. This society has also worked out very careful plans

Private work of the Pennsylvania children's aid society extensive.

for investigating applications for children, and for exercising oversight over placed-out children. The Henry Watson children's aid society of Baltimore also has strengthened its placing-out work, and extended its coöperation with institutions, during the past three years. A children's aid society organized in Rochester, in 1895, somewhat on the plan of the Philadelphia society, has done excellent work. A similar agency has been maintained by the Newburgh committee of the New York state charities aid association since 1893, and this association has maintained a placing-out agency at its central office since 1898.

Other aid societies.

In 1885 a society called the American educational aid association, afterwards called the national children's home society, was organized, with an office in Chicago. Although placing out was not its original object, it found this a more attractive field, and founded a number of state organizations for such work. The society soon became a loose federation of state organizations whose work differed greatly in character and merit. Societies were organized in some states already amply provided with placing-out agencies, and the character and methods of the promoters of the national organization were not always such as to com-

The national children's home society, a loose federation of placing-out organizations, not all reliable.

mend themselves to thoughtful people. In
some cases the state organizations passed
into the hands of incompetent, if not untrust-
worthy, people. In other states much good
has been accomplished and more careful
methods have been introduced. The Illinois
branch has recently been reorganized, and
with the aid of its efficient secretary has done
and will do much to improve the situation in
that state. The work of the Minnesota, Ohio,
Wisconsin, and South Dakota branches has
also been commended. The organization as
a whole has done much to popularize the
placing-out plan, and has created a public
opinion in its favor which has had a favorable reflex action upon many public and private institutions. Beginning in Illinois in
1899, it has been active in securing legislation concerning children in many states.

Its influence as a whole favorable for placing out and children's legislation.

The boys and girls' aid society of California
was organized in San Francisco in 1874 to
undertake the work carried on so successfully
by the New York children's aid society. It
has, however, devoted most of its energies to
the maintenance of a temporary home for
children.

In 1885 a boys and girls' aid society was
organized in Portland, Oregon. This society
has a temporary home for the reception of des-

titute and neglected children, from which they are placed out as soon as possible. During 1900, 380 children were received, and the average period of residence in the home was about one month.

In 1898 the Rhode Island nursery association, organized in 1890 to care for destitute infants, closed its institution and adopted the boarding-out system. After three years' experience it is strongly in favor of the latter system.

Since 1895 several states have enacted laws regulating the placing out of children in families in those states by societies incorporated in other states. Such legislation sprang in part from a belief that crippled, diseased, deformed, feeble-minded, or incorrigible children were being placed out in some of the western states from the large eastern cities, becoming in many instances, it was alleged, public charges, and that in some instances children were placed in improper homes. Another reason was the belief on the part of the local placing-out agencies that their opportunities for placing out children were diminished by the placing of children in families in their states from eastern cities. Owing to grave doubt as to the constitutionality of a law prohibiting the "importation

Restrictions on placing out from other states enacted in several states.

of children," legislation has taken the form of regulation, such regulation sometimes being so rigorous as to amount in practice to prohi-

Michigan. bition.   Michigan passed a law in 1895 requiring all associations or individuals wishing to place a child from without the state in a home in Michigan to file a bond of $1000 that such child shall not become a public charge before it shall have reached the age of twenty-one, the bond being forfeited in case the child becomes dependent.   Indiana by a statute of 1899 requires a bond of $10,000, with a forfeit of $1000 for failure to remove any child becoming a public charge, within thirty days after notice of such fact from the state board of charities.   These requirements are such as to be practically

Minne- prohibitory.   In Minnesota, societies from
sota.   other states are required under a law of 1899 to give such guarantee as the state board of charities may require that incorrigible or defective children will not be placed out in the state, and that children becoming public charges within three years after being placed out will be removed.   Illinois in 1899, and Kansas and Pennsylvania in 1901, enacted similar legislation.

The societies and institutions placing out children from the larger cities in the east deny that there has been any occasion for such legislation. Even if careless work had been done by such societies, it is doubtful whether the course followed has been the wisest one for remedying the difficulty. As to the belief that the placing of children in any state diminishes the opportunities of local societies to place out children in that state, this is clearly a supposition, and one which the writer believes to be contrary to the fact. No evidence has been adduced indicating that any state, or any locality in any state, has reached the limit of its natural capacity for absorbing orphan and homeless children into its normal population by placing-out methods.

A method akin to placing out, which has met much success in Boston for the past twenty years, and for shorter periods in Philadelphia, New York, and elsewhere, is that of placing homeless mothers of young children in situations in the country with their children. This avoids making either mother or child a charge upon charity, gives the child the advantage of a mother's care, and the mother the moral benefit of keeping and caring for her child. In Boston this work has been carried on as an individual charity, in Philadelphia by the children's aid society,

Such legislation of doubtful value.

Improbable that any section of the country cannot absorb more homeless children.

Placing out of homeless mothers with young children successfully adopted in the larger cities.

and in New York by the state charities aid association. This association has worked out a careful system of investigation of the homes to which the women are sent, and keeps in touch with them while in situations. It provided 2627 situations for mothers with their babies from the beginning of the work, June 1, 1893, to September 30, 1901.

Among the institutions recently established and worthy of special note is the George junior republic at Freeville, Tompkins county, N.Y. The plan is that of organizing the children in a miniature republic, and thus teaching them the nature and practical operations of government and respect for law. There is also a special currency, a system of payment for services, and of charges for living expenses, by which the children learn by experience the value of labor in securing the necessities and even the luxuries of life, or are made to taste the fruits of idleness. The system affords a wonderfully urgent appeal for self-control, and an unusual opportunity to become worldly wise in the art of living in society. The experiment is of great value in demonstrating the extent to which such methods can be introduced in institutions. Its methods have already been adopted in part in several insti-

The George junior republic, for wayward children.

tutions in Massachusetts and New York. While not distinctly a reformatory institution, the children at the republic are mostly of a class who would otherwise be committed for correctional treatment.

Other lines of improvement in institutional management are suggested by the methods of a group of small endowed institutions which, except as to size, remind one of Girard college, and some of which were doubtless inspired by its example. These institutions are both educational and charitable as to their primary objects, admission being limited to "poor" children. In their organization and administration, however, educational considerations predominate. Among these are the McDonough farm school at McDonough, near Baltimore, receiving boys between ten and fourteen years of age, and the Williamson trade school, Williamson, Pa., near Philadelphia. The latter institution restricts admission to "poor and deserving boys" from sixteen to eighteen years of age, inclusive. In the promising national farm school at Doylestown, Pa., under Jewish auspices, the charity feature is still less evident, admission not being limited to poor boys, though free maintenance as well as free education is

Charitable institutions in which an educational purpose is predominant, mostly endowed.

McDonough farm school.

Williamson trade school.

Jewish national farm school.

provided, and preference is given in admitting inmates to graduates of orphan asylums and similar institutions.

Among institutions for girls, similar to those mentioned above, are the Foulke and Long institute of Philadelphia, receiving orphan girls from eleven to eighteen years of age, the Samuel Ready asylum for orphan girls, of Baltimore, and the Egenton female orphan asylum, also of Baltimore. The Samuel Ready asylum, opened in 1887, has an endowment of half a million dollars and valuable real estate. Admission is by competitive examination. The girls are admitted at from five to fourteen years of age, are kept until eighteen, and are taught dressmaking, typewriting, bookkeeping, music, and other means of earning a livelihood. The Egenton asylum, opened in 1880, receives an annual income of $10,000 from its endowment. It, too, aims to receive the more promising class of orphans, from four to eight years of age, and to give them special training. It is contemplating removal from the city to the country.

When we pass to such institutions as Hampton and Tuskegee, in which the pupils, all over sixteen years of age, pay, by cash or labor, for their board and lodging, receiving

Foulke and Long institute.

Samuel Ready asylum.

The Egenton asylum.

Hampton and Tuskegee.

free of charge only their instruction, we may consider that we have left charity behind, and are in the ranks of strictly educational institutions.

The Cincinnati children's home, the Cleveland protestant orphan asylum, and, to a less degree, the Chicago orphan asylum, have laid special stress upon the temporary care of children, and placing them in families at an early age. The Rose orphans' home at Terre Haute, Ind., and the Washburn memorial orphan asylum of Minneapolis have paid greater attention to institutional care. In Chicago there are now twenty-three homes and asylums for children supported by private donations, a large majority of which have been founded since 1875. There are also in or near the city four "industrial schools," two for boys and two for girls, largely supported by public funds, and one foundling asylum.

The number of institutions and societies for caring for poor children, founded by private enterprise and maintained by private charity, is so large that it is not possible even to mention many excellent and notable institutions. Scarcely a city of any size in the whole United States is now without some organized effort in behalf of destitute children.

Other institutions.

In connection with the census of 1880, Mr. F. H. Wines prepared a list of homes for children in each state, with their census on June 1, 1880. This list of 613 institutions, with a total population of 50,579 children, appears in the *International Record of Charities and Correction*, March and April, 1886, and a summary by states may be found in the proceedings of the national conference of charities and correction of that year.

Census of children in institutions, excepting reformatories.

In the census of 1890, part ii of the report on crime, pauperism, and benevolence, p. 882, also by Mr. F. H. Wines, the number of inmates of institutions for children, not including reformatories, is given by states but not by individual institutions. There is also a table (pp. 894 ff.) giving the census of each benevolent institution in the United States, but it includes hospitals, homes for the aged, and other charities, as well as homes for children, and in many cases it is impossible to determine the purpose of the institution from its name.

The following table, compiled from the census returns of 1880 and 1890, includes both public and private institutions for the care of children, but does not include reformatories nor children in families:

NUMBER OF CHILDREN IN CHARITABLE INSTITUTIONS IN THE UNITED
STATES, AS SHOWN BY U. S. CENSUS IN 1880 AND 1890.

	Number of institutions	Number of children	
North Atlantic Division	1880	1880	1890
Maine	6	198	196
New Hampshire	5	144	256
Vermont	2	176	203
Massachusetts	45	3,463	3,263
Rhode Island	7	319	522
Connecticut	11	466	728
New York	127	18,624	22,653
New Jersey	20	1,049	1,574
Pennsylvania	69	7,339	8,278
	292	30,778	37,673

South Atlantic Division			
Delaware	3	118	163
Maryland	27	1,653	1,459
District of Columbia	11	—	818
Virginia	13	354	380
West Virginia	2	69	74
North Carolina	2	162	212
South Carolina	7	397	439
Georgia	13	461	502
Florida	1	4	16
	79	3,218	4,063

	Number of institutions	Number of children	
North Central Division	1880	1880	1890
Ohio	47	4,149	5,970
Indiana	18	915	1,762
Illinois	21	1,453	2,703
Michigan	14	747	1,144
Wisconsin	12	656	1,117
Minnesota	5	126	897
Iowa	3	190	568
Missouri	24	1,643	1,613
North Dakota ⎱ South Dakota ⎰	1	—	—
Nebraska	—	—	111
Kansas	2	55	161
	147	9,934	16,046
South Central Division			
Kentucky	18	950	819
Tennessee	10	362	605
Alabama	5	226	340
Mississippi	3	149	156
Louisiana	20	1,991	1,682
Texas	4	206	473
	60	3,884	3,975
Western Division			
Colorado	—	—	212
New Mexico	1	—	107
Nevada	2	187	49
Washington	2	—	184
Oregon	4	69	105
California	26	2,509	3,237
	35	2,765	3,894
United States (total) . . .	613	50,579	65,651

In view of the fact that in New York alone the number of children in institutions (not including reformatories) has increased to 32,600, the total census of children's homes in the United States in 1900 may be conservatively estimated at from 80,000 to 85,000, or, including juvenile offenders (numbering 11,107 in 1880, and 14,846 in 1890), at 100,000. We can only guess at the number of children who have been placed in families, and now are (or ought to be) under the supervision of public authorities or public or private institutions or societies. If we were to venture an estimate we should place the number at not less than 50,000. It is to be regretted that, so far as can now be ascertained, there will be no statistics concerning destitute, neglected, or delinquent children in the census of 1900.

A total for the United States of probably nearly 100,000.

CHAPTER XI

DELINQUENT CHILDREN

Historical sources and discussion: The best available literature is in the proceedings of the national conference of charities and correction, especially for 1875, 1880, 1883, 1885, 1888, 1890, 1894, 1896, and 1897. " Juvenile reformatories in the United States," T. J. Charlton, in " The reformatory system in the United States " (Government printing office, 1900). " Boys as they are made, and how to remake them," F. H. Briggs (Rochester, 1894). " A half century with juvenile delinquents, or the New York house of refuge and its times," B. K. Pierce (Appleton, New York, 1869). As to classification see " Classification of children needing care, training, or reformation," W. P. Letchworth, April, 1882 ; " Classification and training of innocent and incorrigible children," the same, proceedings national conference, 1883; also, " Girls' reformatories, reasons for establishing a separate girls' reformatory, etc.," the same (Matthews, Northrup, & Co., Buffalo, 1887). See also industrial training of children in houses of refuge and other reformatory schools, W. P. Letchworth (Argus Co., Albany, 1883). Annual reports of the trustees of the Lyman and state industrial schools (State house, Boston); house of refuge, Glen Mills, Pa.; state industrial school, Rochester ; house of refuge, Cincinnati; industrial school for girls, Middletown, Conn.; state industrial school for girls, Adrian, Mich.

AT the opening of the century there was not in existence in the United States a single institution for the reformation of juvenile delinquents ; children convicted of offences were committed to jails and prisons, along with adult offenders. The history of juvenile reformation during the century may be epitomized in a sentence, — the removal of youthful offenders from association with adults, and their treatment from an educational and reformatory, instead of a punitive, point of view.

Trend of the century's work for juvenile delinquents.

The first institution for juvenile delinquents in this country (several were in existence in Europe) was established in New York city. On December 16, 1817, several prominent citizens met at the New York hospital to consider the prevailing causes of pauperism. Two months later they organized the "society for the prevention of pauperism." This society wisely considered, very early in its deliberations, the condition of the various city institutions, and in its second report, dated December 29, 1819, attention was called to the fact that in the Bellevue prison, located on the same grounds as the almshouse and city hospital, no separation was made between mature and juvenile offenders. The report says, — "Here is one great school of vice and desperation; with confirmed and unrepentant criminals we place these novices in guilt, — these unfortunate children from ten to fourteen years of age, who from

Origin of the New York house of refuge, 1824.

neglect of parents, from idleness or misfortune, have been doomed to the penitentiary by condemnation of law." After asking, "And is this the place for reform?" the report makes a recommendation, which, though at that time a notable step in advance, would now raise a storm of indignation if proposed in any one of our forty-five states. It proposed the erection, at moderate expense, of a building within the penitentiary enclosure, for the youthful convicts. The recommendation was not, however, carried into effect, and subsequent reports reiterated the folly of committing children to prison along with hardened offenders.

The annual report of the society in 1823 was devoted almost wholly to this subject, and advocated the establishment of a house of refuge for juvenile offenders, after their discharge from prison. In June, 1823, upon the motion of Isaac Collins, afterward prominently connected with the Philadelphia house of refuge, a committee was appointed to prepare and report at a later meeting a detailed plan for a house of refuge, and such a plan was submitted on December 19, 1823, at a public meeting. The purposes of the institution as outlined in this report were:

1. To furnish, in the first place, an asylum

in which boys under a certain age, who become subject to the notice of our police, either as vagrants, or houseless, or charged with petty crimes, may be received. . . .

2. The committee have no doubt that were such an institution once well established and put under good regulations, the magistrates would very often deem it expedient to place offenders in the hands of its managers, rather than sentence them to the city penitentiary.

Purposes of the house of refuge.

3. A third class, which it might be very proper to transplant to such an establishment and distribute through its better divisions, are boys, some of whom are of tender age, whose parents are careless of their minds and morals, and leave them exposed in rags and filth to miserable and scanty fare, destitute of education, and liable to become the prey of criminal associates.

4. Youthful convicts, who on their discharge from prison, at the expiration of their sentence, finding themselves without character, without subsistence, and ignorant of the means by which it is to be sought, have no alternative but to beg or steal.

5. Delinquent females who are either too young to have acquired habits of fixed depravity, or those whose lives have in general been virtuous.

The meeting decided to form a society for the reformation of juvenile delinquents, and $800 was subscribed for its purposes. The active workers in the society for the prevention of pauperism became members of the new society, and the old organization ceased to exist. The following March, 1824, the society was incorporated by a special act of the legislature. Application was made to the city council for a grant of land, and a site containing about four acres, including the space now lying between Fifth and Madison avenues, from Twenty-third to Twenty-sixth streets, which had been ceded to the federal government to be used as an arsenal, was transferred to the society for the sum of $6000, of which $4000 was subsequently remitted. This site was then about a mile from the outskirts of the city, and was surrounded by farms. Here, in the old soldiers' barracks, on January 21, 1825, the first institution for the reformation of juvenile delinquents in the United States was opened, six girls and three boys having been brought in by the police to be cared for. Immediately upon the opening of the institution the construction of a separate building for girls was begun, and it was dedicated on Christmas day, 1825. The state legislature had made

✓

Provision made for both boys and girls.

an appropriation of $2000 to the institution in 1825; in 1826 an act was passed authorizing the institution to receive children from any city or county in the state, and providing that the commissioners of health should pay to the institution any surplus from their funds not required for the maintenance of the marine hospital. For the first five or six years contributions were taken up at the annual meetings, and collected from early subscribers, but after that time the receipts were wholly from public sources, state or municipal.

Income practically all from public funds.

It appears that very early in its history the plan of sending children to the west was in vogue. The daily journal kept by the superintendent contains the following entry for May 10, 1828 : "We saw the eight boys for Ohio start in good spirits. . . . It excited considerable warm good feeling to see so many little fellows bound for such a good and suitable place from the house of refuge, among the passengers on board the steamboat."

Placing out.

In an interesting report " On the penitentiary system in the United States," made by the French writers, Beaumont and de Tocqueville, who visited the United States in 1833, considerable space is devoted to the New York,

Boston, and Philadelphia houses of refuge; the plan of the New York institution is commended, though the results as stated would not be considered very encouraging at the present time. The visitors made an inquiry as to the conduct of all the children who had left the refuge, and reported that, "Of 427 male juvenile offenders sent back into society, eighty-five have conducted themselves well, and the conduct of forty-one has been excellent; of thirty-four the information received is bad, and of twenty-four very bad; of thirty-seven among them the information is doubtful; of twenty-four rather good than otherwise, and of fourteen rather bad than good. Of eighty-six girls who have returned into society, thirty-seven have conducted themselves well; eleven in an excellent manner; twenty-two bad, and sixteen very bad; the information concerning ten is doubtful; three seem to have conducted themselves rather well, and three rather bad than otherwise. Thus of 513 children who have returned from the house of refuge in New York into society more than 200 have been saved from infallible ruin."

By 1839 the growth of the city had reached the institution, and it was proposed to open Twenty-fifth street through its grounds. As a result this site was abandoned, and what

Character of the institution's work.

had been known as the Bellevue fever hospital, with a block of ground between Twenty-third and Twenty-fourth streets, extending from First avenue to the East river, was given by the city for this purpose. On October 10, 1839, the children were removed to the new institution. In the report of this year it is remarked that the children are retained for an average period of one year, at a per capita expense of $1.27 per week.

Ten years later, in 1848, the 355 inmates of the institution exceeded considerably its proper capacity, and a committee was appointed to consider the best mode of providing additional accommodations, and also of securing better classification. In 1850 the committee reported in favor of a change of location, and an application was made to the state legislature for aid to erect two buildings. The city gave its consent to the sale of the property at Twenty-third street and East river and the use of the proceeds towards the purchase of another site. Ten and one half acres of land on the west shore of Ward's island were first purchased, but before steps were taken for its improvement an exchange was made with the city for thirty acres of rocky and marshy land on the south shore of Randall's island. The legislature appro-

Removed to Randall's island, 1854.

priated $50,000 for the erection of new build-
ings, the cornerstone of which was laid November 24, 1852. In an address on this
occasion one of the speakers stated, alluding
to the "nursery for destitute children" maintained by the city on the same island, "We
mean to be good neighbors, only we intend
to compete with them in the supply of apprentices, and gain, if we can, the reputation of
furnishing the most useful and best behaved
children. Our formidable wall of enclosure
will protect our children from the contamina-
tion of theirs, or *vice versa*, as the case may
be." The sale of the Twenty-third street
property realized nearly $175,000; the re-
mainder of the total cost of $470,000 was
met by the state. On the last day of October, 1854, the inmates, 400 in number, were
removed from Twenty-third street and East
river to the Randall's island buildings, which
the institution still occupies. This combination of city aid, state aid, and private control
now proves to be a serious embarrassment,
since it has become desirable to remove to a
country site, with larger opportunities for
agricultural training and with buildings
erected upon the cottage system.

Though this institution was the pioneer in
the field, and has always remained under the

management of some of the most distinguished citizens of the metropolis, it did not continue to lead in the work which it had so nobly begun. During the last quarter of the century other institutions have taken the van in such improvements as the abandonment of the system of contract labor (which was strongly upheld by a manager of this institution at a national conference of charities and correction in 1883); the abolition of the cell system; the introduction of industrial training for purposes of instruction; and the partial or complete abolition of corporal punishment. It is a singular fact that this institution, controlled by a private corporation, the managers of which have always been among the most respected citizens of New York, has failed to keep pace, in these directions, with other institutions, many of which are controlled by managers appointed by governors of states, or other public authorities.

This institution, under private control, has failed to keep pace with other public and private institutions.

The second juvenile reformatory in the United States was a strictly municipal institution, the house of reformation for juvenile offenders, established by the city of Boston in 1826, and located in a portion of the building of the house of correction for adult offenders. In 1837 it was removed to a separate building, but still near the house of

Boston established a municipal house of reformation in 1826.

correction. In 1840 a committee was appointed to consider the wisdom of having both boys and girls in the one institution. Dr. Samuel G. Howe reported for the committee and in favor of separation. He was of the opinion that "the number of happy cases of reformation may be increased by (1) placing children with virtuous families in the country as soon as possible after their committal, and without waiting even for them to be taught to read and write in the house" (this he did not consider practicable in all cases), and (2) "by so administering the house that there shall be more classification." The decision in favor of the removal of the girls was complied with, but in the following year, on the recommendation of the superintendent, who believed that he "could reform boys and girls, too, in the same house," they were readmitted.

During the early years of its existence the house of reformation was the subject of much discussion, suffering almost equally from ill-considered praise and from unmerited odium. It was the subject of frequent changes of government and of organization. By some it was regarded as so desirable a school for boys that parents endeavored to have their children placed there without legal or just cause.

Again, it was represented as a prison of severe character, and unceasing efforts were made to procure the discharge of boys, even when committed for serious offences. In 1841, on account of various criticisms which had led the courts to commit but few children, the abandonment of the institution was proposed, a large part of the buildings being unoccupied. It was at this time that the institution was placed under the control of the directors of the house of industry. In 1846 we learn that, during the preceding two years, the older boys had been employed by contractors at light shoe-making, which had yielded a revenue of nearly $1000 a year. In 1851 the commitment of truants to the house of reformation was authorized; a few years later the managers complained that the institution had become crowded with truants, committed for from three to six months only. The house of reformation was removed to Deer island in 1858, and in 1860 a separate building for the girls, also on the island, was provided. In 1889 the department for girls was closed, all wayward girls being sent thereafter to the state institution at Lancaster. In 1895 the boys' department was removed from Deer island to Rainsford's island. It remained under the charge of the same city officials as

This institution has suffered much from changes of government and organization.

the juvenile and adult paupers and offenders until 1897, when a separate department for children was established. The institution has always suffered seriously from its association, both territorially and in the public mind, with institutions for the care of adult paupers and prisoners. For many years the best public opinion of Boston has favored its removal from the island to a country location, but thus far a sufficient public sentiment to enable the city to make this desirable change has not been secured. The trustees of the children's institutions department strongly urged the change in their report for 1900, and in 1901 legislation was secured authorizing removal to the mainland, within or outside of the city, and the change of the name to "Suffolk school for boys," both changes being subject to the approval of the city authorities by a two-thirds vote. Such approval has not yet been given.

Association with adult pauper and correctional institutions harmful.

Efforts to remove to a country site so far unsuccessful.

The third juvenile reformatory in the United States was the Philadelphia house of refuge, the first meeting for the organization of which was held February 7, 1826. The institution was opened November 29, 1828. In its organization it followed very closely the plan of the New York institution. The board of managers was a private corporation, and

Philadelphia house of refuge, 1828.

has so continued to the present, though under the present law, of the twenty-eight managers, two are appointed by the mayor and three by the court of common pleas of Philadelphia county. At the opening of the institution the fact was emphasized that it was not to be a prison, but "a work of charity and mercy; the refuge is not a place of punishment; it is not a provision simply, or even principally, for the security of society against offences by the confinement of the culprits, or for inflicting the vengeance of society upon offenders as a terror to those who may be inclined to do evil. In the accents of kindness and compassion it invites the children of poverty and ignorance, whose wandering and misguided steps are leading them to destruction, to come to a home where they will be sheltered and led into the ways of usefulness and virtue." After remaining at the original site for twenty years, the house of refuge was removed to Twenty-second and Poplar streets, which was then a rural district. From here the boys' department was removed in 1892 to Glen Mills, Delaware county, Pa., to a farm of 410 acres and to buildings erected on the cottage system. The girls' department remains at Twenty-second and Poplar streets, in the city. At present and for some years

Removal of boys' department to Glen Mills.

the cost of maintenance has been divided about equally between the city of Philadelphia and the state. The fact that the institution is under the control of a private corporation, though doubtless of great advantage in many ways, is probably something of a drawback, as it is also in New York city, in securing needful appropriations for additional buildings. During the past year the legislature was asked for a special appropriation for an additional cottage for the boys, and at the same time the managers endeavored to raise by subscription funds for erecting another building in the girls' department. It is significant, however, that two years ago one of the managers gave to the institution a splendid gymnasium, drillroom, and swimming pool, probably a more serviceable building for these purposes than would be provided by any state or municipal administration. Here, as in another institution referred to later, a separate cottage for the younger boys was provided during 1898. A news sheet, the *Glen Mills Daily*, is issued every day except Sunday. The industrial schools of the Philadelphia institution have taken high rank during the past decade. Comparatively little use is made of the placing-out system : of 423 boys discharged

Private control, with public maintenance, in some respects a drawback

during 1900, 324 were returned to friends; thirty-eight were indentured; forty-three were discharged by order of court or were returned to court; ten were discharged "to find work"; two on recommendation of physician; one to an almshouse; and five died. A careful system of visitation is, however, maintained over the boys indentured, as also over those returned to their parents. The indenture system would not seem to be very satisfactory, from the fact that of the thirty indentured children who passed from the oversight of the visiting agent during the year, four were returned to the institution, fifteen absconded, and only eleven remained until the maturity of the indenture. Of the inmates discharged from the girls' department, the proportion of those indentured is somewhat larger. In the removal to a country site, the separation of the boys' and girls' departments, the development of industrial training for purposes of instruction, and in the relaxation of the former severity of discipline, this institution has taken an advanced position.

The next juvenile reformatory was not founded until seventeen years later, when the boys' house of refuge was established as a municipal institution by the city of New Orleans. It was opened in 1847, receiving

Most of the children returned to relatives.

Noteworthy features of the institution's work.

New Orleans house of refuge, 1847,

sixteen boys that year. The census increased rapidly, and in 1857 was 182. A girls' department was added in 1852, but was subsequently discontinued. The boys' department remains a municipal institution, but has passed through many vicissitudes, and has become rather more a lodging and boarding house for homeless boys and vagrant boys committed for short terms than a reformatory. So far is it from meeting the needs of Louisiana in this direction that a strong effort was made in 1901 to establish a state reformatory for boys. Although the bill was not passed, the board of control of the prisons was authorized to establish such an institution whenever the funds of the state will permit.

of little real value in reformatory work.

In 1847 the Lyman school for boys was established by the state of Massachusetts, upon the suggestion of Hon. Theodore Lyman, ex-mayor of Boston, who gave to the state a considerable sum for this purpose. The institution was, however, from the first, strictly a state institution in its management, and was the first of this character in the United States, if not in the world. We are told that several cities, Lowell, Worcester, Cambridge, and others, had established reform schools in connec-

The Lyman school for boys, 1847, managed by the state of Massachusetts.

tion with their almshouses, but these institutions were probably of the character of homes for destitute and neglected children rather than of juvenile reformatories. The institution was located at Westboro, where it still remains. In accordance with Mr. Lyman's suggestion the commitments to the school were during minority, and were limited, except in special cases approved by the trustees, to children under fourteen years of age; the upper age limit was, however, soon extended to sixteen, with an alternative sentence for a less period to the house of correction or other penal institution. Many inmates preferred a shorter sentence in a penal institution, and attempted to secure such transfer by bad conduct in the reform school. In 1859 the alternative sentence was abolished; a school-ship or nautical branch was established, and the age for commitment limited to fourteen. Many of the children upon leaving the school were indentured to persons approved by the trustees, but they were not visited. When the state visiting agency was established in 1869, it found great opportunity for improvement in the selection of families, and thenceforth a report from the visiting agent was required before a child was placed in a family.

Age limits.

In 1879 the boards of trustees of the state charitable institutions were abolished, and the state reform school for boys, the state industrial school for girls, and the state primary school were placed under one board, the trustees of the state primary and reform schools. After the abolition of the school-ship in 1872, the reform school for boys suffered from a change in the law, requiring it to receive boys up to seventeen years of age. This was repealed, however, when the Concord reformatory was established in 1884. The reform school for boys was thenceforth known as the Lyman school for boys. It was removed to a different site, without walls or enclosed yards, and with buildings on the cottage system; the age for commitment was limited to fifteen years. A careful oversight is now maintained over children who have been indentured, and a few of the younger children are boarded in families, with the alternative of a return to the school if they misbehave. The Lyman school has carried the cottage system more nearly to its logical conclusion than most boys' reformatories; its cottages are smaller, more homelike, and more widely scattered; it emphasizes manual training in addition to trade teaching, and personal and moral influences rather than institutional meth-

The cottage system adopted.

ods; and individualizes the treatment of its
inmates to a marked extent. It has justly
earned the confidence of the people, and
occupies a very high place among reform
schools for boys in the United States.

Individual treatment.

Two years after the establishment of the
Lyman school, the western house of refuge
in New York, a purely state institution, located
in Rochester, was opened. At first this was
an institution for boys only, girls from all
portions of the state still being sent to the
institution in New York city. The first
superintendent of the Rochester institution
had for five years filled the corresponding
position in the house of refuge in New York
city. The Rochester institution was for
many years not unlike most institutions of
its class. During the past fifteen years,
however, it has made very rapid advances in
introducing modern methods of discipline, and
more especially in the development of its
industries and in the teaching of trades, in
which it was a pioneer. Its site, owing to
the growth of the city of Rochester, has become too valuable to be longer used for such
purposes, and its buildings are of obsolete
type. Under legislation of 1899 a commission selected a country site for the institution. The necessary legislation for its

The western house of refuge, New York state, of late years emphasiz-ing trade teaching.

purchase in 1900 was not secured, nor was a similar bill in 1901 successful. It is still hoped, however, that the removal may be made within a very few years. It would be very desirable if the girls' department of the state industrial school of Rochester and that of the house of refuge could both be discontinued and a separate institution for wayward girls established.

Need of a separate institution for girls.

One year after the establishment of the western house of refuge at Rochester, the first juvenile reformatory west of the Alleghany mountains was founded by the city of Cincinnati. This institution was established, and is still conducted, on the congregate system, and is one of the best of the reformatories on that system. It has laid special emphasis on its industrial department, and has not developed to any great extent its placing-out work.

Cincinnati.

In 1851 Pennsylvania, following the example set by New York two years earlier, established the house of refuge of western Pennsylvania, at Morganza. This was at first a voluntary association, but subsequently the counties in the western judicial district of Pennsylvania were authorized to subscribe not exceeding $10,000 each to the building fund of the institution; and each county so

House of refuge of western Pennsylvania,

subscribing was authorized to appoint one manager for every $2500 subscribed, such managers to be in addition to those selected by the voluntary association. The institution was at first located in the city of Allegheny, but in 1872 was authorized to move to a country site, not more than fifty miles distant from Pittsburgh, and moved to Morganza, Washington county. In 1875 the statute was amended so that the power of appointing managers was vested solely in the governor, except as to such managers as were then appointed by the counties that had contributed to the building fund. The voluntary membership was abolished, and the institution became strictly a state institution. The cottage system was adopted by this institution when it removed from the city of Allegheny to its country location in December, 1876. The boys and girls are divided into eight families. The institution receives about one third of its support from the state, and two thirds from the counties from which its inmates are received.

under combined state and county support.

The boys' house of refuge was organized in Baltimore in 1849 and opened in 1855. In its government it was curiously complex, ten of the twenty-four managers being appointed by the mayor, ten by the subscribers

House of refuge of Baltimore.

to its funds, and four by the governor. Its support was likewise partly state, partly municipal, and partly private. This institution early laid great stress on its educational work. A girls' department was maintained until the separate female house of refuge was established. Manual training was introduced in 1891, both state and city making appropriations for this purpose. The placing-out system was worked out more carefully than was common with such institutions.

The reform school for boys opened at Lancaster, Ohio, in 1856, introduced the new type of institution variously known as the open, cottage, or family system. The object was to introduce more of the features of family life, to encourage self-control by placing greater reliance upon the boys, and to separate them into grades, on the basis of character and conduct. This school was a pioneer in these directions, but its example was followed in many states, and has taken precedence over the earlier congregate plan.

The Ohio school at Lancaster, a pioneer in the cottage system.

The New Jersey reform school for boys was opened June 28, 1867, as a state institution. Its early reports speak in favor of many features which were not then commonly regarded with favor, but which are now very generally accepted. Its first report states that " The system which it is proposed to adopt is to have families of boys in separate houses, each family to be under the care of a suitable man and his wife. The advantages of the plan are, briefly, that such division awakens more of the interest and affections of home in the minds of the boys, and places them permanently under the notice and supervision of the parents of the house, who, devoting themselves to their own pupils, acquire a more perfect acquaintance with and influence over them than could be the case were they in congregate establishments like the refuges of metropolitan cities." The same report describes a "system of grading which puts the character of each boy in his own hands." It states also that although the open farm system offers almost unlimited freedom, there had been but one attempt to escape, and that was unsuccessful.

This system adopted also by the New Jersey school.

It is to be noted that the managers of this institution, before adopting its plans for building and management, conferred especially with the authorities of the Ohio reform school, and that the first superintendent had an intimate acquaintance with the workings of the state reform school at Westboro, Mass. Subsequent reports speak in high terms of the success of the open-farm system and the system of grades or credits and demerits. The placing-out system is also spoken of as in considerable use with excellent results, in the report of 1869.

The rapid multiplication of juvenile reformatories after 1850 precludes further mention of individual institutions; it will be noted, however, that a much larger proportion of institutions for wayward children are public, *i.e.* under state or municipal control, than of institutions for destitute children. The majority are strictly state institutions, though there are a few municipal institutions of this nature, nearly all of which were established prior to 1875. Even in states in which the contract or subsidy system prevails for the care of destitute children, the juvenile reformatories are usually under public control. The general tendency is indicated by the conversion in 1899 of the Maine industrial school for girls, which hitherto had been a private institution receiving state aid, into a state institution with a board of trustees appointed by the governor. There are a few reformatories under private control and supported by private funds, such as the Berkshire industrial school, located at Canaan Four Corners, N.Y., and others. There are also

The tendency toward state control.

numerous convents under the charge of religious sisterhoods, for the reformation of young women, several of which also receive girls.

A list of juvenile reformatory institutions in the United States is given in the United States census of 1890. A list is also given in a paper by Mr. T. J. Charlton, contributed to "The reformatory system in the United States," prepared for the international prison commission by Hon. S. J. Barrows, and published as a state document in 1900. From these lists and other sources the following list has been compiled. Institutions established primarily for adults, or which receive also a large proportion of destitute children, are not included.

List of juvenile reformatory institutions.

1824   House of refuge, New York city.
1826   House of reformation, Boston.
1828   House of refuge, Philadelphia.
1845   Boys' house of refuge, New Orleans.
1847   Lyman school for boys, Westboro, Mass.
1849   State industrial school, Rochester.
1849   House of refuge for boys, Baltimore.
1850   House of refuge, Cincinnati.
1851   Reform school, Morganza, Pa.
1853   State reform school, Portland, Me.
1854   State reform school for boys, West Meriden, Ct.
1854   House of refuge, St. Louis.
1856   State reform school, Lansing, Mich.

1856   Boys' industrial school (formerly called "the reform farm"), Lancaster, Ohio.

1858   State industrial school, Manchester, N.H.

1858   State industrial school for girls, Lancaster, Mass.

1860   State industrial school for boys, Waukesha, Wis.

1864   State reform school, Jamesburgh, N.J.

1864   The house of the good shepherd, Baltimore.

1865   Industrial school of reform, Louisville.

1866   Reform school for boys, Plainfield, Ind.

1866   Reform school, Vergennes, Vt.

1867   Industrial school for boys, Eldora, Iowa.

1867   Female house of refuge, Baltimore.

1868   St. Mary's industrial school for boys, Carroll, Md.

1869   Reform school, Washington.

1869   Girls' industrial school, Delaware, Ohio.

1869   Industrial school for girls, Mitchelville, Iowa.

1870   Industrial school for girls, Middletown, Ct.

1870   House of reformation for colored boys, Cheltenham, Md.

1870   Plummer farm school, Salem, Mass.

1871   State industrial school for girls, Trenton.

1871   Reform school for girls and women's prison, Indianapolis.

1873   Newark city home, Verona, N.J.

1874   Industrial school for girls, Hallowell, Me.

1875   Industrial school for girls, Milwaukee.

1878   State industrial school for girls, Adrian, Mich.

1878   State reform school, Red Wing, Minn.

1880   State industrial school, Golden, Col.

1880   State reform school, Topeka.

1880   State industrial school, Kearney, Neb.

1882   Oaklawn school for girls, Howard, R.I.

1882   Industrial home for colored girls, Melvale, Md.

1883   Sockannosset school for boys, Howard, R.I.

1885   Ferris industrial school, Wilmington, Del.

1886   Berkshire industrial farm, Canaan Four Corners, N.Y.

1886   State reform school, Nashville.

1888   Reform school for boys, Boonville, Mo.

1888   State industrial school for girls, Chillicothe, Mo.

1888   State industrial school for girls, Beloit, Kas.

1888   State reform school, Plankinton, S.D.

1889   State industrial school, Ogden, Utah.

1890   State reform school, Pontiac, Ill.

1890   Laurel industrial school, School P. O., Va.

1890   Girls' industrial school, Geneva, Neb.

1890   Whittier state school, Whittier, Cal.

1891   State reform school, Chehalis, Wash.

1891   State reform school, Turner, Ore.

1892   State home for juvenile offenders, Geneva, Ill.

1892   The house of the good shepherd for colored girls, Baltimore.

1892   Preston school of industry, Waterman, Cal.

1893   Reform school for girls, Washington.

1894   Delaware industrial school for girls, Wilmington, Del.

1894   Montana state reform school, Miles City, Mont.

1895   State industrial school for girls, Montclair, Col.

1897   Virginia manual labor school, Hanover, Va.

1897   Industrial home for girls, Salem, W. Va.

1899   Industrial school for white boys, East Lake, Ala.

1900   State reformatory for boys (white and colored), Marianna, Fla.

1900   State reformatory for girls (white and colored), Marianna, Fla.

1901   State home for delinquent boys, Illinois.[1]

1901   Territorial reform school, Arizona.[1]

1901   Reform school for boys, New Mexico.[1]

1901   State training school for girls, Red Wing, Minn.

Several general tendencies in juvenile reformatory work are obvious. It is interesting to notice the various names by which reformatory institutions have been known at different periods. At first they were houses of refuge. Then it was sought to emphasize the object of the institutions by calling them reform schools. In course of time this name came to have its disadvantages. To have come from a reform school was not a good recommendation; in fact, it was a distinct handicap to the discharged pupils. To escape from this, and also to emphasize the industrial features, the name industrial school was taken up. As this came to be more and more generally used, it came to have some of the disadvantages of "reform school," and it also had an unfortunate effect upon industrial schools that were not reformatory in purpose. Probably the best solution is that of giving the school the name of some person or place.

Evolution of the titles of reformatory institutions.

[1] Established by legislature of 1901; site not yet selected.

This neither creates a false impression, nor makes prominent the reformatory feature. The Michigan institution has been named by statute successively, "house of correction," "state reform school," and "industrial school for boys."

The importance of employment as a means of preventing deterioration, and as a positive reformatory agency, was early recognized. At first the industries were extremely simple. In some cases the labor of the inmates was farmed out to contractors by the hour, or by the piece. This gradually gave way to manufacturing industries carried on in the institution under the direction of its own officers, and for the production of articles for consumption in the institution, or for the market. This in turn, in the best institutions, has been replaced by the introduction of industries for the purposes of instruction rather than of revenue. Those industries that are most useful in producing revenue are apt to be less useful in fitting a boy for outside life. Some, notably chair-caning and brush-making, came to be known in the industrial world as "institution" industries. For this reason, among others, in his report in the national conference of charities and correction of 1890, Mr. T. J. Charlton said of chair-caning,

Employment at contract labor or at manufacture under officers of the institutions gives place to industries for purposes of instruction.

— "I must confess that I dislike this industry more than any other that has been mentioned in this report." There is also an excellent paper on the same subject by the same writer in the conference proceedings of 1897. The best reformatories are industrial schools in fact as well as in name.

In the construction of buildings, the cottage plan is clearly preferred. Though congregate institutions still are built, they find no defenders, except on grounds of economy. Discipline has more and more relaxed in severity. Bolts, bars, and high walls are rapidly becoming things of the past. In 1898, of forty-three reformatories reported upon at the national conference of charities and correction, thirteen were classed as "walled" and thirty as "open" institutions. Though the terms were not very clearly defined, these figures undoubtedly fairly represent the preponderant sentiment in favor of the open system. More and more the problem is seen to be primarily one of education, not of repression, or even of reformation, as that term is ordinarily used. The evil tendencies are to be attacked indirectly by the introduction of new interests, new ambitions, and new powers.

One of the most striking evidences of in-

The cottage plan,

open grounds,

and education, not repression, the modern tendency.

creasing discrimination and of more careful classification in the treatment of juvenile delinquents is the rapid extension during the three years, 1899 to 1901 inclusive, of the probation system. This system involves, either in terms or in effect, a suspension of sentence, the child being permitted to return to his own home, there to remain under the oversight of a probation officer, and subject to further court proceedings in case of misconduct. The probation officer is expected to keep informed of the child's conduct, to aid him if necessary in securing and keeping employment, and to act in general as adviser, friend, and protector. Probation thus combines the giving of "one more chance" to the boy who has faced the prospect of being deprived of his liberty, the holding over him of the continuing possibility of punishment for deeds already done if his conduct fails to be exemplary, and, most important of all, the advice, encouragement, and assistance of a presumably experienced, wise, and discreet friend.

Reformation without institutional confinement: the probation system.

Probation work was one of the prominent features of the state visiting agency established in Massachusetts in 1869. It probably had been in operation to a limited extent prior to that date, the children being placed

under the care of benevolent individuals will-
ing to assume the responsibility. With the
establishment of the state visiting agency,
having a representative in court at the trial
of all juvenile offenders, there came both the
opportunity of systematically urging that
juvenile offenders be placed on probation in
suitable instances, and of placing them under
the oversight of an organized department
with salaried officers. The matter is considered quite fully in the first and second annual
reports of the state visiting agent, included
in the seventh and eighth annual reports of
the board of state charities of Massachusetts,
1869–70 and 1870–71. From 1870 to the
present a table showing the total number of
trials of the juvenile offenders in the state,
and the disposition made of them, appears
in the reports of the state board of charity.
During the first fifteen months of the existence of the agency, of the 799 juveniles tried,
189, or twenty-three per cent, were placed on
probation. During the following year, of
1463 cases, 456, or thirty-one per cent, were
placed on probation. The report of the
agency for that year states that the magistrates were placing increased numbers on
probation, " being aware that the future well-
being of such children would be promoted, if

Marginal notes: The system in Massachusetts since 1869.

Results of the first year's work.

not secured, by the subsequent action of the
agency in visiting and guiding them, and
surrounding them with more healthful influences than they had previously enjoyed. As
an influence for restraining and reforming
our probationers we have called to our aid
various religious and benevolent organizations,
both catholic and protestant." Only thirty-
nine of the 456 placed on probation came
again before the courts, or became obnoxious
to the officers of the law during the year.

The percentage of juvenile offenders placed
on probation has varied from nineteen to
thirty-three per cent. The figures for various
years are as follows:

	Total cases	Number placed on probation	Percentage placed on probation
1869–70	799	189	23
1871	1463	456	31
1875	2775	542	19
1881	1178	344	29
1885	1701	606	33
1890	2079	500	20
1895	3105	791	25
1900	3750	709	19

Percentage of offenders placed on probation.

When the visiting agency was abolished in
1879, its probation work along with its other
work was transferred to the state board of
health, lunacy, and charity; but from that
date or shortly thereafter, the agents of the

state board have acted as advisers of the judges in the disposition of juvenile offenders, in some cases giving nominal surety, but have not undertaken personal visitation and oversight of children during a probationary period. Subsequently local probation officers, representing the courts, were appointed. In 1878 the first law was passed requiring the appointment of a probation officer for the city of Boston. In 1880 a law was passed for the whole state authorizing the aldermen of each city, and the selectmen of each town, to establish the office of probation officer; this law was permissive only, and little was accomplished under it. In 1891, largely as the result of the efforts of the secretary of the prison commission, a law was enacted requiring the criminal courts throughout the commonwealth to appoint such officers, and defining their powers and duties. These local probation officers act for both juveniles and adults. In Boston one or more private societies also appointed agents to attend the trial of juvenile offenders, and in suitable instances to offer to exercise an oversight over juvenile offenders whose cases were continued for definite periods, such agents giving nominal surety. The effect of this is to put the children on probation, their cases being placed perma-

Development of the system.

Court probation officers made mandatory, 1891.

nently on file or otherwise disposed of at the end of such periods. The Boston children's aid society has employed such an agent since February 1, 1889.

The value of probation work in Massachusetts was admitted, but, while without doubt in many places and on many occasions wise judges have given convicted boys "another chance" and have asked discreet friends to "look out for" those so favored, the system did not secure formal adoption, so far as we are aware, in any other state until the enactment of the juvenile court law in Illinois in 1899. This law authorized the appointment of probation officers and the commitment of children to their care. Several different charitable societies assigned one or more of their salaried officials to the juvenile court in Chicago as probation officers. A number of police officers also were assigned to this work, serving in citizens' clothing. The city was districted and one district assigned to each probation officer. The Chicago juvenile court with its probation system attracted attention and study from many quarters. The Illinois children's home and aid society was largely instrumental in securing the legislation, and the children's home societies of many other states urged the passage of similar laws, in

Illinois adopts the system in 1899.

several instances successfully. The visitation and aid society, a Roman catholic society for placing children in families, devoted its monthly periodical, the *Juvenile Record*, to an account of the operations of the juvenile court, and advocated the establishment of a similar court in every state in the union.

At this time (1901) the probation system is in actual operation, or is provided for by statute, in fifteen of the twenty-five largest cities of the United States. Rhode Island in 1899 empowered the state board of charities to appoint a person to act as probation officer throughout the state, and in its discretion to appoint additional such officers, of whom at least one must be a woman. Courts were authorized to commit juvenile or adult offenders to their care. Three such agents were appointed during 1900. One hundred and ninety boys between ten and sixteen years of age were committed to one of these officers, of whom only twenty were returned to the court during the year. Another agent looks after the adult males; the third cares for women and girls. The probation system was adopted in 1899 in Minnesota for the three counties having more than 50,000 inhabitants, the officers being nominated by the state board of

Probation now recognized in fifteen of the largest cities of the country.

Rhode Island.

Minnesota.

charities and confirmed by the judges of the
district court of the county and receiving a
salary from the county treasuries. In 1900
a permissive probation law was enacted in
New Jersey, under which a probation officer New
was appointed in Hudson county (Jersey Jersey.
City) on June 1, 1900. His first annual report showed that 121 persons, of whom
seventy-two were boys and three girls, had
been committed to his care. Of the seventy-
two boys only four violated their parole during the year. The law was also carried into
effect in Essex county, and perhaps elsewhere. In 1901 the probation system was
adopted, as a part of the juvenile court law,
in Pennsylvania, Kansas, and Wisconsin.
The Pennsylvania law applies to the entire Other
state, is mandatory, and has already been states.
put in operation in Philadelphia; the Kansas law is permissive; the Wisconsin law
applies only to the one county (Milwaukee)
having a population of more than 150,000,
and, while mandatory as to requiring a separate court, is permissive as to the appointment of probation officers. Special laws for
probation work were secured in 1901 for the
cities of Washington and Buffalo. In Washington the board of children's guardians des-
ignates one of its employees as a probation

officer; in Buffalo the officers are unpaid. In New York a general law took effect September 1, 1901, providing for the appointment of probation officers throughout the state, but the law is made inapplicable to children under sixteen, except in the city of Buffalo. Missouri passed a carefully prepared probation law, applicable only to the city of St. Louis, in 1901.

New York.

An important step in securing better classification and wiser discrimination in dealing with neglected and delinquent children has been the establishment of separate courts to deal exclusively with children's cases. This not only prevents the actual association of children with adult offenders, but also makes possible a much more satisfactory system of records, helps to bring about a reasonable degree of uniformity in dealing with children, and promotes coöperation between the various agencies for assisting children. In 1869 the Massachusetts statute establishing the state visiting agency required that children's cases should be "heard and determined, by themselves, separate from the general and ordinary criminal business of said courts." Similar legislation, but permissive in form, was enacted in New York in 1892, in Pennsylvania in 1893, and in Rhode Island in 1898,

Children's courts, to dissociate children from adult offenders, and systematize their treatment.

It remained for Illinois, however, to establish the first court devoted exclusively to children's cases and held entirely apart from courts dealing with adults. This was established in Chicago under the provisions of the juvenile court law of 1899.[1]

Illinois establishes the first exclusively children's court, 1899,

[1] The number of children tried before the juvenile court during the year ending June 30, 1901, was 2378, as follows:

Dependent boys	543
Dependent girls	528
Total dependents	1071
Delinquent boys	1075
Delinquent girls	129
Total delinquents	1204
Discharged as neither dependent nor delinquent	103
	2378

The disposition made of the dependent children was as follows:

Committed to training schools and other institutions	517
Committed to societies for placing children in families	86
Committed to Illinois humane society	19
Committed to societies and individuals for adoption	4
Returned to parents under care of probation officers	445
	1071

The disposition made of the delinquent children was as follows:

and is
followed
by other
states.

A similar law was enacted in Pennsylvania in 1901, a juvenile court being opened in Philadelphia in July of that year. A law of 1901 requires a separate children's court in Milwaukee. The revised charter of New York city, taking effect January 1, 1902, provides a separate court for such of the children's cases as are now heard in the seven different magistrates' courts. That the example of these large cities will be widely followed can hardly be doubted.

Committed to John Worthy school (the city reformatory for boys attached to the house of correction) 662
Committed to other institutions 99
Held to the grand jury 12
Released in care of probation officers . . . 431
                                                                ———
                                                                1204

Of the delinquents, in addition to the 431 placed on probation without commitment, 658 were placed on probation on their release from the John Worthy school, — a total of 1089 delinquents placed on probation during the year. Of this number 195, ten and one half per cent, were returned to the court for further proceedings during the year.

CHAPTER XII

PRESENT TENDENCIES

THE experience of the century and the increasing study given to child-saving work during the past twenty years might naturally be expected to result in more or less clearly defined tendencies toward the wider adoption of some methods, and the modification or rejection of others. Through the free competition which has prevailed, or, if that phrase sounds harsh as applied to charities, through the unrestricted opportunity for each system to demonstrate its inherent tendencies and to secure its natural and logical results, certain methods should by this time have shown their fitness to survive. Are we able at the opening of a new century to see any signs pointing toward the general adoption of certain methods ?

As to governmental agencies, the facts are evident. As between state *versus* county, city, and town systems, the state plan is far in the lead. No new states are establishing a series of local or county homes for children.

Of public agencies, the state system is in the lead.

It is doubtful whether any one of the three states that have county children's homes would choose this plan if they were now for the first time establishing their system. The increasing effectiveness of state supervision over the county homes, approximating in some cases actual control, suggests the probability of state management in the not distant future. State management would certainly be followed, sooner or later, by a sharp reduction in the number of the institutions.

The real contest, if such it may be called, will be between the state and the contract or subsidy systems. To put it plainly, the question now being decided is this, — shall our state administrations be intrusted with the management of a system for the care and training of destitute children, or is it wiser to turn that branch of public service over to private charitable corporations, leaving to public officials the functions of paying the bills, and of exercising such supervision over the workings of the plan as may be possible? Each of these plans finds new advocates and wider adoption yearly. Strongly contrasted in spirit and method, and, in any one state, almost mutually exclusive, it seems probable that one plan or the other will, by a process of gradual selection, gain the ascendency, and

The contest is between this and the contract system.

become distinctively, though probably not exclusively, the American system of public care of destitute and neglected children. Which it shall be, only the twentieth century can tell. Each plan is yet susceptible of much improvement, each has powerful advocates, and each has behind it some of the most influential factors in American social and political life.

There are some indications that in the country as a whole the state system will gain in favor more rapidly than any other. No state that has adopted it has abandoned it; nor in any state in which a state system has been actually established has there been any movement in favor of its abandonment or serious modification. On the other hand, the contract or subsidy system seems to be as a rule in a state of unstable equilibrium. Opposed as it undoubtedly is to the natural instincts of many American people, and containing in itself tendencies to an undue growth, which inevitably alarm still others who are not opposed to it from principle, it arouses from time to time efforts for its better regulation. These, if successful, naturally and properly strengthen its hold on public favor, but if they fail, one after another, lead to a demand, which in more

Indications that the state system will prevail, but not exclusively.

than one case has prevailed, for its abolition. There is little reason for thinking that the contract plan will ever be wholly discontinued in all the states, but, for the reasons above stated, it seems likely that it will not make much further progress, and that it may be discontinued in some localities in which it is at present in operation.

As to the form which the state systems are likely to take, there undoubtedly is a growing tendency to create a strong central state unsalaried board of several members, having to deal only with children's work; to vest in this body the custody of all destitute and neglected children in the state who are public charges; and to leave the board in a large measure free to work out the best system for caring for the children, through temporary institutions, boarding out, and placing out. After all, the essential difference between the Massachusetts state system and the Michigan plan is simply that for the temporary care of children the latter uses an institution, while the former uses boarding out. In both plans the placing of children in free permanent homes is the chief feature. Already there are evidences that the Michigan, Minnesota, and other similar institutions are finding a limitation of their plan, evidenced

An unsalaried state executive board probable, to deal exclusively with children's work, by boarding out, temporary institutions, and placing out.

by the gradual accumulation of children who are not available for placing in free homes, such as crippled, unattractive, slightly diseased, and other cases. These must either accumulate in the institution, as seems to be the case in Minnesota, or be returned to counties and refused admission to the state school, as is the case in Michigan, where already there is a movement either to compel the state school to receive such cases or to create a new state institution for them. Many of these children could be placed in families at board, though not, for some time at least, in free homes. For this reason, and also because as communities grow older the opportunities for placing children who are too old for legal adoption seem to grow less, it is likely that the state systems will gradually find it desirable, if not necessary, to place certain of their children in families with payment for board. Whether the state schools for dependent children will follow the example of the state of Massachusetts and the city of Boston in doing away with the temporary institutions altogether, is doubtful.

Children who cannot be placed out may be boarded out.

Several tendencies in the management of private charities for children are evident. The older orphan asylums are in some cases still conducted on nearly the same lines as

Private institutions recognizing the value of placing out and boarding out.

when first organized, but among the newer institutions there is almost a general acceptance of the fact that orphans and children upon whom there is no valid parental claim are much better off if adopted by families, and that to rear them in asylums until they are twelve, fourteen, or sixteen years of age is an expensive, wholly unnecessary, and seriously harmful, blunder. This sentiment found expression in the unanimous report of the committee on the care of destitute and neglected children to the national conference of charities and correction in 1899. The very general sentiment in favor of placing children in free homes in families is likely to lead to a more general adoption of the boarding-out plan by private charities, as the limitations of the plan of placing out without payment for board are more clearly perceived, and as such limitations become more pronounced as communities grow older.

Cottage plan preferred to the congregate.

In the institutional care of all classes of children, the cottage plan has clearly proved its superiority to the congregate system. Those who continue to erect congregate dormitories must be ready to apologize for them to the enlightened sentiment of the community.

The general movement in favor of industrial education leads naturally to a pronounced tendency to provide trade teaching in institutions, for such of the older children as, for good and sufficient reasons, are retained. It is now seen, however, that this training is simply that which should be within the reach of all children, and that it can be offered to children living at home, or with other families, as easily as to those living in institutions. We are not likely to have many more institutions founded for the express purpose of teaching trades, which make residence in the institution and support from its funds a necessary condition for receiving such instruction. Philanthropists who wish to further the cause of industrial education are more likely to follow the example of Pratt, Drexel, Armour, and Auchmuty, than that of Girard and Williamson. Such children as must be kept in institutions will be given every practicable opportunity for industrial training, but children will not be gathered into institutions for the purpose of giving them such training.

As to the division of the field between public agencies and private charities not receiving public aid, little change is noticeable, except an increasing tendency to regard the public authorities as the appropriate agencies to assume the care of children who are to be

Trade teaching should not be institutionalized, but available for children living at home.

Public authorities for permanent

permanently separated from their families, and private charities as more particularly fitted to deal with those cases involving temporary assistance, or the care of children for whom some payment is made by a surviving parent. Associated charity, individual effort, and private funds have never done more for destitute children than at present. There need be no fear that they will be rendered unnecessary by the development of a state system.

Nor, unfortunately, does there seem to be any reason for thinking that charities for caring for destitute, neglected, and delinquent children will soon become unnecessary. We learn to deal more and more wisely with those who are in distress, but the forces which produce poverty, neglect, and crime seem to be beyond our reach. The poor, the neglectful, and the vicious we shall have with us for a long time to come, and the hearts of the generous will continue to respond, both through individual and associate charity, and through governmental action. There is ground for rational optimism, however, in the fact that, more and more, thought is added to kindliness, and that, as surely as experience and study bring fresh truths to light, so surely does the intelligent sentiment of the community, sooner or later, compel their adoption.

charges; private charities, for temporary assistance.

The need of charitable effort not diminishing.

Public sentiment compels the adoption of approved methods.

INDEX

Almshouse care: prevalent, 3; in large cities, 4 ff; in counties, 7; 12; New York, 13 ff; Philadelphia, 23 ff; Boston, 29 ff; Massachusetts, 33 ff, 157; New York state, 37 f; condemned, 38 f; removal from almshouses, *see* chapter iv; number of children in almshouses, 80 f.

Baltimore: 6; 10; 41; Baltimore orphan asylum, 49; St. Mary's orphan asylum, 50; Watson children's aid society, 68; house of refuge, 219.

Bethesda orphan house, Savannah, 9, 45.

Binding out, *see* indenture.

Boarding out: 6; 7; 21 ff; 24; 63; 68; 70; chapter viii; 242; 244.

Boston: 6; 10; 29 ff; house of industry, 29; children's asylum, 30; house of reformation, 29, 31, 207 ff; Deer island, 31; farm school society, 49; boarding out, 154 ff; children's aid society, 69 f, 182 ff.

Boston farm school society, 49.

Brace, Charles Loring, 66.

California: contract system, 131 ff; boys and girls' aid society, 186.

Centralized *vs.* local administration, 3, 239 f.

Charleston orphan house, 7, 32 f.

Chicago: private institutions, 193; probation system, 233; children's court, 237.

Children's aid societies: 65 ff; New York, 66 ff, 182; Baltimore, 68, 185; Boston, 69 f, 182 ff; Brooklyn, 71; Buffalo, 71; Pennsylvania, 71, 140, 184.

Children's courts: Illinois, 165, 237; other states, 236 ff.

Children's guardians, boards of: District of Columbia, 137; New Jersey, 163 f; Indiana, 177.

Children's home society, 185 f.

Cincinnati house of refuge, 218.

Classification of children, 148 f, 229.

Colorado: state home, 92; humane society, 178.

Colored orphans, 59.

Commitment, methods of: 11;

247

17 f; 26; 29; 35; 62; Michigan, 84, 95; Connecticut, 107; New York, 125, 129 f, 174 f; District of Columbia, 137; Massachusetts, 152 f, 158; Illinois, 165; neglected children, 171.

Commitment of children obviated, 128.

Connecticut: removal of children from almshouses, 78, 80; county home system, 106 ff.

Contract care of paupers: prevalent, 3; disuse, 13, 38.

Contract system for care of children: 109; chapter vii; 239 ff.

Cottage plan, 113, 216, 220 f, 228, 244.

County children's home system: chapter vi; 239 f.

Cruelty, societies for prevention of, 170, 172 ff.

Delaware: 7; subsidies, 141.

Delinquent children: chapter xi; 190.

Disposal of asylum inmates, 64; see placing out, etc.

District of Columbia: subsidy system, 135 ff; board of children's guardians, 137 f.

Education, compulsory, effect on institutions, 65.

Endowed asylums, 57 ff, 191.

Family vs. institution training, 67, 244.

Farming out: prevalent, 3; disuse, 13, 38.

George junior republic, 190.

Girard college, 57 f.

Heredity, influence of, 88.

Humane societies, 173.

Illinois: almshouse care, 80; children's law of 1899, 165; children's home and aid society, 186; probation system, 233; children's court, 237.

Indenture: prevalent, 3, 8; New York, 22; Massachusetts, 34 f; visitation of children, see this title; decadence of, 39 ff; 46 f; 67.

Indiana: 41; removal of children from almshouses, 79; county home system, 109 f; children's guardians, 177.

Indian children, 60, 118.

Infants, 6, 21, 22 f, 24, 62 f.

Institutions, census of children in, 194 ff.

Iowa, state home, 93.

Kansas, state school, 91.

Local vs. centralized administration, 3, 38, 239.

Maine, subsidies, 141.

Maintenance combined with education, 59.

Maryland: 7; 8; 10; 40; removal of children from almshouses, 78; subsidy system, 139 f.

Massachusetts: 8; 33 ff; state primary school, 34 f, 151 ff;

state visiting agency, 34 f, 151, 231; indenture, 39; removal of children from almshouses, 73 f, 83 : boarding-out system, 150 ff, 242; neglected children, 167, 169; Lyman school, 214 ff; probation system, 229 ff.

Michigan : removal of children from almshouses, 74 f; state school system, 83 ff, 98, 242; neglected children, 170 ; placing out restricted, 188.

Milwaukee, subsidy experience, 141 f.

Minnesota: state school system, 87 f, 99 f, 242; placing out restricted, 188; probation system, 234.

Missouri, 164, 166.

Montana, state home, 92.

Mothers with children placed out, 189.

Municipal care of children : Charleston, 7, 32; New York, 13 ff; Philadelphia, 23 ff; Boston, 29 ff; vs. state care, 239 f.

Natchez protestant orphan asylum, 50.

Nebraska, children's institution, 94.

Neglected children: 10; chapters ix, x.

Nevada, state orphanage, 92.

New Hampshire: removal of children from almshouses, 78; state supervision of children, 143 f.

New Jersey: removal of children from almshouses, 79; board of children's guardians, 163 f; reform school, 220 f; probation system, 235.

New Orleans: 9; Poydras orphan asylum, 50; house of refuge, 213.

New York catholic protectory, 63.

New York city: 5 f; 8; 9; 11; 13 ff; Bellevue, 13 ff; Long Island farms, 16 ff; Randall's island, 19 ff; Blackwell's island, 19; foundlings, 23; indenture, 41; orphan asylum society, 45 ff; R. C. orphan asylum, 50; juvenile asylum, 61; catholic protectory, 63; children's aid society, 66, 182; contract system, 118 ff; foundling hospital, 124; society for prevention of cruelty, 172 ff; house of refuge, 199 ff.

New York juvenile asylum, 61.

New York orphan asylum society, 45 ff.

New York state: 8; 35 ff; removal of children from almshouses, 75 f; subsidy system, 116 ff; rules of state board of charities, 125; neglected children, 168 ff; house of refuge, Rochester, 217.

North Carolina, subsidies, 141.

Ohio : removal of children from almshouses, 73; county home

system, 103 ff; Lancaster reform school, 220.

Oregon: subsidy system, 140; boys and girls' aid society, 186.

Outdoor relief: prevalent, 3, 4; diminution, 12; Boston, 29; condemned, 36 f.

"Pauper" stigma, 146.

Pennsylvania: 7; 8; removal of children from almshouses, 77 f; children's aid society, 77, 159 f; subsidies, 140, 159; boarding out, 159 f; western house of refuge, 218.

Philadelphia: 4; 10; 23 ff; children's asylum, 24 ff; Blockley almshouse, 27 f; orphan society, 50; Girard college, 57; boarding out, 160 f; house of refuge, 210 ff.

Placing out: chapters v and viii; 64 ff; 104; 107; 110; 119; 123; 129; 143; 176; 182 ff; restrictions on, 187 f; mothers with children, 189 f; 193; 244; see also indenture and boarding out.

Politics in institutions, 97 ff, 145 f.

Poor law, English, in America, 3.

Private charities for children: chapters iii, ix, x; 8 ff; list of private charities, 52 ff; types of institutions, 55 ff; tendencies, 243 f.

"Private" defined, 12.

Probation system, 229 ff.

Public care of children: chapters ii, iv, v–viii, xi; 3 ff;

Yates report, 35 ff; state systems classified, 82; see also state care and municipal care.

"Public" defined, 12.

Reformatories, list of juvenile, 223 ff.

Relief: systems in use in 1801, 3; of widows, 9; outdoor relief, see this title.

Religious institutions, 56 ff; 60 f; 120 ff; 141; 162; 182.

Retention in institutions, 18; 26; 46; 64 f; 120; 123; see also temporary care.

Return of children to parents, 18, 26, 108.

Rhode Island: removal of children from almshouses, 78; state school system, 90, 100; probation system, 234.

Savannah, 9.

Society for the relief of poor widows with small children, New York, 9, 45.

Soldiers' orphans, 101.

State care of children: chapters ii, iv, v, viii, xi; Massachusetts, 33 ff; New York Indians, 60; classification of state systems, 82; delinquents, 222; vs. the contract system, 239 ff.

State school system, chapter v.

States without systems of public care, 166.

Subsidies to private charities: 47 f; 62; 64; 77; 83; 91; 94; 102; chapter vii; 159; 175; 180; 239 ff; see also contract system.

Temporary care of children, 63, 70, 78, 95, 107, 175, 180, 193, 245 f.

Tendencies in the care of children: chapter xii; delinquent children, 226 ff.

Tennessee, subsidies, 144.

Texas state asylum, 93.

Trade teaching, 57, 92, 191 f, 227 f, 245.

Ursuline convent, New Orleans, 9.

Virginia, 8.

Visitation of placed-out children: Massachusetts, 34; Michigan, 84 f.

Washington: orphan asylum, 50; see also District of Columbia.

Wisconsin: removal of children from almshouses, 77; state school system, 89, 100.

Yates report on public care, 35 ff.

This biography is reprinted from the
"Encyclopedia of Social Work"
(Washington, D.C.: National Association of Social
Workers, 1977), pp. 485-486.

Homer Folks

(1867–1963)

For over half a century, Homer Folks did unique and distinguished work in the organization and administration of public health programs for the prevention and treatment of tuberculosis and mental illness, the improvement of public welfare administration, aid to dependent children, and probation.

Folks was born in Hanover, Michigan. He received a BA from Albion College in 1889 and from Harvard College in 1890. Following graduation from Harvard, he became general superintendent of the Children's Aid Society of Pennsylvania and continued in that position until 1893.

Folks's achievements were primarily identified with the State Charities Aid Association, an organization of private citizens in New York State that worked for improved health and welfare services. He became secretary of SCAA in 1893 and served continuously until his retirement in 1948, except for a term of office as commissioner of public charities of New York City, 1902–03, and a period abroad with the American Red Cross, 1917–19.

During his years with SCAA, Folks played a leading part in the public health movement. In 1907 the association under-took a cooperative program with the New York State Health Department for the pre-vention and control of tuberculosis. This program was one of the most successful and comprehensive efforts of its kind in the United States. As a result of legislation that established a series of county tubercu-losis hospitals and clinics and provided for the employment of public health nurses, the tuberculosis death rate in New York State sharply declined.

As executive officer of SCAA, Folks also administered health demonstration proj-ects on the prevention and treatment of tuberculosis in a rural county and a medium-sized city in upper New York State. Similar demonstration projects were undertaken by the SCAA in cooperation with the state health department for the prevention of venereal disease and the control of diphtheria in young children through immunization.

Under Folks's leadership the SCAA's State Committee on Mental Hygiene con-tributed to many improvements in the state's programs for the mentally ill, including the establishment of outpatient clinics and the employment of trained personnel. He served as a member of the National Com-mittee for Mental Hygiene and as chairman of important state committees to study the population of state institutions for the care of the mentally ill.

SCAA's accomplishments in the field of child welfare were equally outstanding. In 1894 SCAA established an agency to help homeless mothers care for their children.

In 1898 it instituted a child-placing and adoption agency that placed thousands of destitute children in permanent homes and established and administered the first of a series of county agencies for dependent children in upstate New York. All these agencies furthered the establishment of high standards of child welfare.

In 1895 SCAA under Folks's direction helped obtain constitutional amendments giving the State Board of Charities increased power to inspect and regulate all state charities, public and private. As commissioner of public charities in New York City during the administration of reform mayor Seth Low (1902–03), Folks reorganized the department and established the first municipal tuberculosis hospital in the United States. He was also active in establishing the Welfare Council in New York City in 1925 and served as chairman of its executive committee for many years.

Folks rendered outstanding service in other fields of social welfare. After the Spanish-American War he spent six weeks in Cuba studying relief needs, and his recommendations were later embodied in that country's charities and public health laws. During World War I he organized and directed the Department of Civil Affairs of the American Red Cross in France; after the war he directed surveys of relief needs in Europe and later coordinated Red Cross activities in the United States.

Folks was appointed vice-chairman and presiding officer of the first White House Conference on Dependent Children in 1909 and participated in successive conferences. He became president of the National Association for the Study and Prevention of Tuberculosis in 1912, the first layman so honored; president of the American Association for the Study and Prevention of Infant Mortality in 1915; and president of the National Conference of Charities and Correction in 1911 and in 1923, when that organization became the National Conference of Social Work. He also served as chairman of the U.S. delegation to the first International Congress of Social Work, held in Paris in 1928.

C. B.

References

Folks, Homer. *Care of Destitute, Neglected, and Delinquent Children.* New York: Macmillan Co., 1902.

"Homer Folks Retires," *American Journal of Public Health,* 37 (April 1947), pp. 493–94.

"Homer Folks, Statesman Emeritus," *American Journal of Public Health,* 37 (May 1947), pp. 570–71.

Zimand, Savel (ed.). *Public Health and Welfare: The Citizen's Responsibility.* Selected papers of Homer Folks. New York: Macmillan Co., 1958.

THE
NASW
CLASSIC
SERIES

The problems we face today didn't begin today. When you travel back in time you gain a valuable new perspective on current issues.

The NASW CLASSICS SERIES is designed to help you do just that. The CLASSICS are paperback reprints of books that haven't been around for awhile, but they deserve to be. The series is dedicated to preserving important literature in the development of social welfare. These "classics," which had a profound impact on their own times, demonstrate how social work grew from a deep-seated charitable impulse into a commitment requiring broad scope and skills.

Order from:
Publications Sales, NASW
1425 H Street, N.W.
Washington, D.C. 20005

Be sure to add 10%
for postage and handling.

Social Work and Social Living

by Bertha Capen Reynolds — *originally published in 1951.*

Bertha Reynold's experiences working with a large labor
union convinced her that the psychologically-oriented
approach of traditional social agencies made it too difficult
for clients to seek help. She demonstrates how social workers
can relate their practice to the actual social situations clients
face. She urges professionals to accept the individual "where
he is," and provide the kinds of supportive treatment that
will help people "mobilize resources within themselves and
in their physical and social environment to meet their reality
or change it."
CBC-071-C Reprinted in 1975. 176 pp. **$3.50**

Social Case Work: Generic & Specific

(A Report of the Milford Conference) — *originally published in 1929.*

By the early 1920s it had become apparent that, even though caseworkers were competent in several diverse areas, the common theoretical base of their practice was not known. The Milford Conference, a group of outstanding practitioners, met several times during the decade to consider the problem. This report, prepared by a special committee of the Conference, reveals the incisive analysis that produced this first important study of casework practice.

CBC-069-C Reprinted in 1974. 92 pp. $3.75

The Dangerous Classes of New York

by Charles Loring Brace—*originally published in 1872.*

The author was one of the first to advocate placement as the preferred method of helping abandoned children and to argue for protective legislation for children. This edition of his famous indictment of poverty includes the original's forceful illustrations.

CBC-061-C Reprinted in 1973. 448 pp. **$5.00**

Social Service and the Art of Healing

by Richard C. Cabot, MD—*originally published in 1915.*

Dr. Cabot, a pioneer in the use of social work as a vital part of medical care, stressed the importance of psychological and sociological factors in treating patients.
CBC-062-C Reprinted in 1973. 192 pp. **$2.50**